Memoirs *of an* Elusive Moth

MEMOIRS

of an

ELUSIVE MOTH

*Disappearing Nightly with
Harry Blackstone and
his Show of 1001 Wonders*

Adele Friel Rhindress

Squash Publishing • Chicago

Memoris of an Elusive Moth

By Adele Friel Rhindress
Edited by David Parr

Copyright © 2011 by Adele Friel Rhindress & David Parr. All rights reserved. No part of this publication may be reproduced or transmitted in any form or by any means, now known or to be invented, without written permission from the publisher.

Jacket design by Kevin McGroarty
Layout and design by Gabe Fajuri

Photos are courtesy the following individuals. The Collection of George Daily: page 38. The Del Ray Collection of Robert Escher: pages 69 and 70. The Robert Parrish Collection, courtesy of David Meyer: Pages 64, 91 and 92. Collection of Willam V. Rauscher: page 6. The Collection of Nick Ruggiero: pages 49, 81, 85, 87, and 96 - 98. Author photo (back flap) courtesy of Joseph Long. All other photographs are from the collection of the author.

Squash Publishing
Chicago, IL 60640
www.squashpublishing.com

ISBN 10: 0-9744681-8-5
ISBN 13: 978-0-9744681-8-1

First Edition
6 5 4 3 2 1

To matinees and nights
and the friends who lived them
— and —
to my daughters and sons,
their husbands and wives,
my grandchildren, great-grandchildren,
siblings, and everyone who ever wanted
to know what it was like

Contents

    Introduction ... ix
    Prologue ... xiii
1 · Enter, Singing and Dancing ... 1
2 · Box Jumping and Other Performing Arts ... 11
3 · Ohio, 1947 ... 19
4 · Born to Dance ... 23
5 · Picture Postcard ... 28
6 · The Elusive Moth ... 29
7 · Pete and Millie Bouton ... 37
8 · Sex and So Forth ... 43
9 · Places and Faces ... 51
10 · Del Ray ... 68
11 · Atlanta, 1949 ... 72
12 · Blackstone Island ... 74
13 · 1001 Wonders ... 80
14 · A Chinese Fantasy ... 94
15 · Exit Stage Left ... 102
    Acknowledgments ... 110
    Blackstone Tour Routes ... 113

Introduction

I might never have seen him.

If somebody hadn't left a copy of the Omaha *World-Herald*, Nebraska's biggest newspaper, in our family car, I would have found out too late.

As a high-school kid I rarely read a newspaper, mainly because there never seemed to be anything interesting — for my world at least — in it unless it was about gymnastics (my sport), or Japan (an odd childhood obsession), or stamps (a side hobby) and mainly nothing about my real hobby. Magic.

Hooked by the purchase of a trick deck of cards (to magicians: a Svengali) at the Nebraska state fair, I branched out from cards to ropes to "apparatus" magic: linking rings, bottle-and-glass exchange, rabbit vanish, etc., astonishing the locals in church basements, Lions Club dinners, and made real money for a high school kid — usually twenty dollars a night and on one memorable occasion an astounding $35 for entertaining a convention of The Future Farmers of America.

But back to that paper.

I decided to see how many movies there were in Omaha theaters, compared with the meager five or six where I lived in Lincoln. Scanning the page, suddenly my eye and brain were grabbed. In a modest-sized print ad, in among similar-looking ones for current and coming movies, the word "Blackstone" swam briefly before my eyes.

Failing to grasp the reality of the moment, my disbelieving brain, in a fragment of a portion of a second, dismissed it. I figured an apartment ad or a law firm's name or, more likely, an ad for the Blackstone Hotel had strayed in among the entertainment ads. That had to be it.

But no. It said "Blackstone, the Magician."

The denial mechanism was working overtime. The ad was among movie ads, so there must be a movie coming about the great magician. That really had to be it. Besides, if Blackstone the Magician were coming it would be a full-page ad, surely. Or maybe announced on the front page.

The earth seemed to move. I saw what it really was. An ad for a Ginny Simms movie. And with Ginny's movie, onstage, Blackstone the Magician. Could this mean in-the-flesh?

It was about breakfast time when this wonder exploded upon me. And a school day. Had it proved to be a one night affair and only that night, I would have headed for the Greyhound Bus Depot, bought a ticket for the sixty-mile trip from Lincoln to Omaha and risked the scandal, doubled because my father taught at my high school.

Still shaken from how close I came to missing the ad and the coming thrill — and how near suicidal I'd have been if someone casually said, "Hey, Dick, I caught Blackstone the other day in Omaha. Where were you?" — I saw that the timing was good. It was the coming weekend and my parents drove me over. We stayed overnight with relatives.

I don't recall how many shows a day alternated with the movie. Could it have been five? I think so. Over the two days, I saw at least that many.

My magician friend Gene Gloye had told me I might be seeing the end of an era. The full-evening magic and illusion show was dying already, throttled in good part by the greed of the musicians' union, he said, whose demands were helping kill that great phenomenon of the entertainment world, the touring show that required an orchestra in the pit.

My folks dropped me mid-afternoon at the theater. Before it all began, part of me was still afraid it was somehow not to be. In those days, when a celebrity came to town, the ad would include the words ONSTAGE! IN PERSON! NOT A FILM! The ad hadn't said that.

I got a chill.

Ginny Simms, a sort of B-rank singing movie star of the time, was onscreen; her vast, heart-shaped Valentine-candy-box face emitting melodies that seemed to go on endlessly and last for hours. I wanted her dead.

After seemingly a week, Ginny warbled her last ditty and the endless movie ended. *Lawrence of Arabia* seemed shorter than that movie. Then there was an infuriating break for refreshment stand revenue. And then the lights went down, the pit orchestra began — I'm pretty sure it was "Who?" — the plush, the grand old classic velvet stage curtains parted — and there he stood. Somehow I got my breath.

He was decidedly not on film. The majestic figure onstage, impeccable in tails and with that bountiful white hair, was in the same four walls as I was. I got goose bumps.

For the next hour or so, I don't think I moved as they came, one after the other: The Crystal Casket, The Floating Lady, Where Do The Ducks Go?, the terrifying Buzz Saw Illusion, the mind-boggling Light Tubes Through The Lady illusion, and maybe best of all, the astounding Floating Light Bulb that, removed from the lamp, kept burning, then hung suspended in air before the magician, and then, after being thoroughly passed over and around in every direction by a solid hoop, floated out among us in the audience.

A lucky kid got called onto the stage for a trick with a rabbit. Blackstone thanked the kid and, before sending the thrilled lad back to his seat, *gave him the rabbit.*

When it was over I headed for the stage door, armed with my eight-by-ten glossy of the great man and a fountain pen of my father's which I had destroyed by filling with some kind of chalky white ink for writing on slick blackness.

I all but smacked into the legendary conjuror just outside his dressing room. He was all graciousness and signed my picture. I told him that I too was a magician. "Don't neglect to practice," he advised and I promised. All a-twitter, I thanked him, reluctantly left his presence and then realized, out on the street, that I didn't have the pen.

I went back. He asked, amusedly, if I had come for one more autograph. When I said I was afraid he had kept my pen, he smiled and said, "I put the pen in your pocket."

And he produced it from my shirt pocket. Whether it had been there or not, I'll never know. I prefer to think I got one more bonus trick out of Harry Blackstone.

Dick Cavett
May, 2011

Prologue

In her other life, she was a moth — an elusive one.

Night after night, she spread her wings and danced through the jungle, voodoo drums throbbing in her ears, savage tribe in hot pursuit behind her. And night after night they would catch her in the gigantic web of a spider, and hoist her into the air so she could not escape.

Yet escape she did.

A flash of light, a burst of smoke, and she was gone — vanished, just as though it were a magic trick.

Of course it *was* a magic trick. It was The Elusive Moth, an illusion performed by Harry Blackstone. For three seasons, from 1947 to 1950, Adele Friel was an assistant in the big, spectacular Blackstone magic show. Afterward, she married, added Rhindress to her name, raised a family, and now, these many years later, she looks back to give us an inside glimpse of what it was like to be part of one of the great magic shows of the 20th century.

If you never saw Harry Blackstone perform, you would find it difficult to imagine the transcendent effect he had on audiences. The combination of superb magic, great humor, overwhelming beauty and spectacle, plus a personality that seemed to say "This is especially for *you*," all worked together to make the Blackstone show one of the celebrated entertainments of its day.

It was not always so, nor had Blackstone always been Blackstone. He was born Henry Boughton in Chicago in 1885. His brother Pete arrived two years later. Shortly after the turn of the century, the two brothers entered show business with a magic act. They played everyplace that would take them — mostly third-class theaters at first, the kind peopled by rowdies and roughnecks. Harry did fast-moving magic; Pete, in grotesque getup, went for the belly laughs by doing slapstick lampoons of it. This is the act that, with its rough edges smoothed, was billed as "Straight and Crooked Magic" on one of their early tours of a genuine vaudeville circuit.

Over the years, they worked under a variety of names, "Fredrik the Great" being one of them. The name got them into trouble during World War I. Anti-German sentiment was widespread in the USA, and people thought that any magician named Fredrik must surely be German. Box office receipts dried up. But if the British monarchy could change its name from Saxe-Coburg to Windsor, why couldn't the magician known as Fredrik the Great change his name to Blackstone? In 1918, that's what he did. Box office sales revived, so Blackstone he remained.

Something else changed besides the name. Humor was never absent from the show, but greatly improved bookings soft-pedaled Pete's slapstick shenanigans. He has been taking over more and more responsibility for the physical equipment of the show and now he made that, and backstage supervision, his full-time job. For time to come, Harry would be the front man, and Pete would reign behind the scenes.

By the time Adele Friel joined the show in 1947, it was nearing the end of its fifty-year career. It had grown from a rag-tag slam-bang diversion by two feckless young blades into an elegant, elaborate, full-fledged theatrical production that advertised a cast of thirty. Its steady climb had included thousands of performances in everything from vaudeville to carnivals to a showboat, from military posts to elegant theaters to movie houses, and everywhere in between.

Blackstone's notable feats of magic included The Vanishing Horse, in which a real live equine disappeared by magic; Broadcasting a Human Being, during which a young lady was "transmitted" from one place to another, supposedly via air waves; the Bridal Chamber illusion, in which a lady's boudoir magically materialized, complete with bed, side table, lamp, real Siberian wolfhound, and a living "bride"; The Girl From the Tires, which featured a dazzling woman appearing from a stack of automobile tires that the audience had seen piled one on top of another; and The Old Man with the Whiskers, in which the magician invisibly changed places with another character.

When Blackstone Senior died, his son took up the wand. Harry Blackstone Junior launched a show that, in addition to his own gifted magic, featured many of his father's wonders. When Harry Junior died in 1997, it was the end of the Blackstone era.

There are many fine magicians working today. Rightly, they style their shows to today's sensibilities. The memoirs of Adele Friel Rhindress take us to an important time in magic and a crucial time in American life. They give rare insights into such things as the bigger-than-life figure that was Harry Blackstone, how a major touring magic show was run, what went on backstage, the staging of certain illusions, the secrets behind some of them, the extraordinarily busy life of assistants (male and female), and the unique experience of trouping, all of which must surely ring bells for anyone who is on the road — or who wants to be — today.

Daniel Waldron
Author of *Blackstone: A Magician's Life*

MEMOIRS *of an* ELUSIVE MOTH

1 · Enter Singing *and* Dancing

Blackstone? Never heard of him.

That's right. I never had, even though in 1947 — the year I first became aware of that name and the man behind it — he was the most famous magician in America, and his *Show of 1001 Wonders* was the most famous touring illusion show.

I was seventeen years of age, and must confess that I was oblivious to almost everything except the song-and-dance act of Adele Friel — me. I'd been dancing professionally since I was sixteen, working weekends at Philadelphia nightclubs, hotels, conventions, and dinner shows. By age seventeen and graduation from high school, I had gained the happy reputation of being "a solid act" and I could work full time. I was never the star, but I often opened for budding entertainers such as Orson Bean, Jerry Vale, Jack Klugman, Ed McMahon, and others who went on to become widely known in their day.

I loved the work. I loved dancing. It was immensely satisfying, especially since it meant that I could contribute to my family's income. My father, Bill Friel, was earning $75 a week — a respectable sum in those days — as a sergeant of police at the Philadelphia Naval Base. My mother, Isabel, was a registered

"Doll Dance" Nightclub act publicity photo, taken at age 16.

nurse. But the money didn't go far when there were four growing children to raise. I was the oldest, so I felt a special commitment to supporting our family.

I did plenty of variety shows, but I'd only worked one show with a magician. It was at a hospital annex for children recovering from surgery, and the magician's name was Doc Irving. At that time, my act included a number in which I wore a doll costume. Doc Irving the Magician asked me if I'd wear my doll costume and toe shoes so I could magically "appear" out of his Doll House illusion. I thought it was a fun idea, so I said yes. The youngsters screamed with delight when a life-size doll popped out of the dollhouse and danced for them. That was my one and only brush with magic.

Until the first week of October 1947.

Harry and Irene Ritter, brother-and-sister theatrical agents I was working with at the time, received an urgent phone call from the Blackstone show, which was playing at Philadelphia's Walnut Street Theatre. They needed a girl — *right now* — to replace one who was leaving the show. The new girl had to fit into existing costumes and illusion boxes. She had to be a quick learner, someone with stage presence, and ready to travel. Harry Ritter lost no time setting up an interview for me. "Adele," he said, "take your portfolio. And good luck."

I smile when I think of that today. Back then, my "portfolio" consisted of three — count 'em, three — publicity photos taken the year before, when I was sixteen, plus a few recommendations from theatrical agents and club owners. Joining a magic show was not really on my list of ambitions — but hey, a gig is a gig, and this one sounded like it might be interesting. The more I thought about it, the more I liked it: *Steady job, maybe. Probably decent pay. A chance to see the country. Could this be my lucky day?*

It was early afternoon when I entered the backstage door at 9th and Walnut streets. I told the guard that I had an appointment with Mr. Blackstone. He checked to make sure I was telling the truth and then ushered me to my prospective employer.

We passed through the backstage area and arrived at a dressing room. There sat Harry Blackstone, reading a newspaper. He looked up and rose to shake my hand. He had large dark eyes, dark eyebrows, a black-and-white mustache, and a mop of wavy white hair. He had a piercing gaze and a very deep voice. He smiled.

A smile is a good start, I thought.

Blackstone and I had a pleasant conversation. He told me what would take place if I were to be hired. He explained about show times, travel schedules, what I could expect and what would be

Harry Blackstone, Sr. poses for a studio portrait.

expected of me. "The members of my show are family," he said. "We help each other, we work together, and we have fun."

The stage manager, Fred Phillips, came in. He gave me the once-over, then said pleasantly enough that if I were hired, he would be available to provide any information or help I needed. "I'm sure you would have a lot of questions," he said. And he was right!

Two girls appeared. Sara Graves was an experienced stage assistant. She wanted to make sure I looked enough like her to act as her "double" in several tricks. We stood next to each other to compare height. She took my hands. We looked each other straight in the eyes. We laughed. She gave me the thumbs up. The other girl, Patty Rose, introduced herself as the person I would be replacing. She was a short-time sub with the show and was going back to Massachusetts to be with her family. Patty explained that there were twelve assistants in the show, six girls and six boys, and a full cast was needed for a show of this size.

That was it. I was hired. The time it took for me to get the gig was no more than ten or fifteen minutes. It was a most unusual job, and I would discover that the man who gave the okay — Harry Blackstone — was a most unusual employer.

Wait until I get home and tell the family!

But I wasn't going home. Not yet. Patty Rose leaped into action. Smiling and talking as we went, she hustled me out the stage door and straight to Baum's, a famous Philadelphia source for costumes, dancing shoes, custom outfits, make-up, and everything for show people. In less than an hour, I had silver high-heeled shoes, the necessities for quick costume changes, a change robe, greasepaint, and a small cosmetics bag to hold my new treasures. Then we hurried back to the theater.

I got a crash course in applying make-up, so I wouldn't "wash out" under the bright stage lights. It was my introduction to The Art of the False Face.

When the spotlight hits you, it drains the color from your face and you can end up looking like a ghost. That might be okay if you're doing a midnight "ghost show" or "spook show," a type of magic performance that was gaining popularity back in those days. Before I joined the show, Blackstone had occasionally presented a special ghost show as a way to draw in publicity and sell tickets. But the *Show of 1001 Wonders* was not about frights in the dark — or under the lights. When we walked onstage, we represented the glamour of magic, so all of us — women *and* men

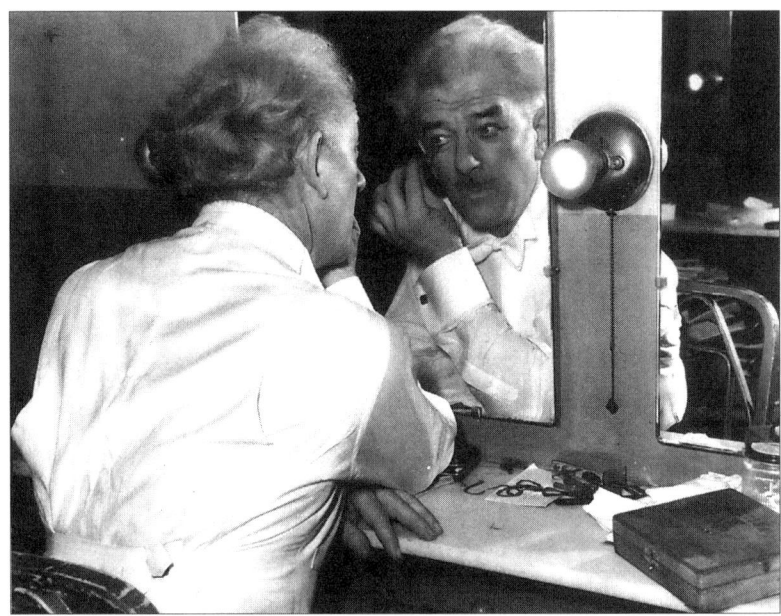

The entire cast, Blackstone included, applied make-up before each show.

— wore stage make-up, and we spent a fair amount of our time applying it.

Stage make-up was different from the make-up I'd used in nightclub shows, and very different from ordinary street make-up. Here's how the Blackstone girls put on their faces.

Supplies were always purchased in the largest size available: big cans of face powder, jumbo tubes of greasepaint, large jars of cold cream. We never knew when we would be able to get to a theatrical supply store, so it was best to stock up when we had the chance. The make-up itself wasn't shared among the cast. Each of us had our own make-up kit and a make-up regimen that was uniquely suited to our individual coloring, facial features, and skin type. Light bulbs around the mirrors in the dressing room gave a good idea of what the make-up would look like onstage.

Our make-up supplies were laid out on a small towel. Tools for applying the make-up were also kept handy: cotton balls, facial tissues, powder puffs, eyelash curlers, eyebrow pencils, lipstick brushes, eyelash brushes. Even so, much of the make-up was applied with the fingertips, starting with cold cream.

After pulling back our hair with a ribbon or cloth tie, cold cream was scooped out of the jar and smeared all over our face and neck. Then, tissues were used to gently wipe it away. A clean face provided a smooth, uniform surface for the greasepaint, which was applied next. The greasepaint was a shade or two darker than our own skin. Its texture was similar to toothpaste. Greasepaint was spread over the face and neck to form an even foundation.

Rouge came next, to accentuate the cheekbones. It was red, of course, and creamy in texture. Using our fingers, we took a dab of rouge out of the can and applied it to our cheeks, starting near the nose and sweeping upward to the outside corners of the eyes. This was followed by a light dusting of powder in the same shade as the greasepaint, all over the face and neck. Excess powder was fanned off so the rouge was visible.

Next, a lipstick brush was dipped into the rouge can, and the rouge was used to make an outline of the upper and lower lips. When the outline was complete, the lips were filled in with lip color. We did not blot or powder our lips, because we wanted them to glisten under the lights.

Some of us finger-dabbed a small amount of rouge on our eyelids for contrast with the blue or brown creamy eyelid color that was applied next. That was in a smaller can than the rouge. The eyelid color was spread gently over the eyelids. Then, brown or black eyeliner was penciled around the edges of the eyes, outlining them. Eyebrow pencil, in black or brown, was used to define the shape of the brows. The eyes and eyebrows are so important for conveying expression and giving the audience a way to connect with the performer. That's why those features were given special emphasis.

The final step was the eyelash curler, to turn the lashes upward and make the eyes look larger. And this is where a bit of alchemy was brought into play. Our make-up kit included a candle, a candleholder, and a box of matches. These were used to prepare an item called "cosmetique." Cosmetique was a cylinder of black wax in a paper tube, about six inches long and approximately as thick as a thumb. A small amount of the wax was placed in a metal teaspoon and held over a candle flame until it melted enough for an eyelash brush to be dipped into it. It had to be applied immediately to the eyelashes. If it hardened too quickly, it was held over the candle again. When the application was complete, each eyelash tip had a tiny ball of black wax on it. This was heavy on the lashes, but it made our eyes look dazzling under the stage lights.

Blackstone and all the male assistants had their own preshow False Face ritual to go through. They had to apply cold cream, greasepaint, rouge, powder, lip color, eyelid color, and eyeliner. But they were lucky: no melted wax on their eyelashes.

With my crash course in make-up completed, Patty Rose listed some of the other backstage procedures. She explained how, before a show, the stage manager would give progressive calls for readiness: "Half hour," "Fifteen minutes," and "Five minutes." At "Five minutes," we were expected to be in our places for the top of the show. At "Curtain," the show would begin.

Patty stood up and said we should run through a quick rehearsal of the tricks I would be working in tonight's show.

Wait. Tonight? They didn't expect me to be in the show tonight, *did they? They couldn't.*

They could and they did. Patty and I went onto the empty stage and she coached me through the routines I would be doing.

I got into boxes and cabinets that looked too small for me to fit inside. I practiced walking with props. I learned how to move quietly backstage in my new high heels. I donned every costume on Earth — or so it seemed! Patty was not a singer, but she hummed the music that went with my routines. We ran through them over and over until I knew the cues for all my appearances and disappearances, as well as the costume changes. There was simply no time to be nervous. We grabbed a bite to eat, and before I knew it, Fred Phillips was calling "Five minutes. Places everyone."

I will never forget that first show. It was a whirlwind. Patty stood alert in the wings and helped me make all my onstage cues and offstage costume changes. My head was spinning, but I made it through. Patty was a good teacher. Tomorrow, though, she would be gone and it would all be up to me.

After the show, I caught the #46 trolley car in front of the theater. It was a half-hour ride to West Philadelphia, then a four-block walk to my family's house. My parents were waiting up for me. I told them all about my interview, how I had gotten the gig, and how Harry Blackstone himself had hired me. I told them that I'd done my first performance that very night. My parents and I had a long, serious talk about the idea of my leaving home to travel with the show, considerations for my safety, hopes for the future. My weekly pay would match my father's salary, and I hoped my expenses would be manageable enough for me to send most of the money home.

I wanted my family to meet Harry Blackstone and the rest of the cast, so we arranged for my parents, my sister Louise, and my brothers Bill and Jack to come see the show at the Walnut Street Theatre. They watched me as I appeared and disappeared onstage. Everyone had a great time.

As the show neared the end of its run in Philadelphia, I thought about what was ahead. After my dance bookings, I had always returned home to sleep in our house and the comfort of my own bed. My life would be different now.

My parents came to see one more show. I told them that it would be at least six months before I saw them again. Tears were shed. Had I been able to glimpse the future, I might have told them that we could all save the emotional goodbyes for another time.

2 · Box Jumping *and* Other Performing Arts

The train pulls into a station in a new town. We grab our carry-on belongings, step off the train, and head for the hotel. Our personal wardrobe trunks will be taken directly there. Costume trunks will go to the theater.

Three railroad cars are necessary to transport the animals, equipment, cast and crew. There are special cars that can be converted to Pullmans — sleeping cars — for overnight travel. Waiting near the tracks are big trucks, ready to haul all of the equipment to the theater. Illusions, props, trunks, all kinds and sizes of boxes and crates, and a menagerie of animals are unloaded from the baggage cars and loaded into the trucks. Every trunk, case and crate is painted bright orange for easy identification. Anything orange belongs to the Blackstone show and will be moved to the theater, along with one exception to the color scheme: a large upright crate on wheels, painted fire-engine red. This red crate is Pete Bouton's portable workshop, with all the tools needed for cutting trap doors in the stage, repairing and maintaining props, providing electrical connections, and handling any other mechanical requirements that might arise. Pete is Harry Blackstone's younger brother. He manages every aspect of the show.

When all of this stuff is delivered to the loading dock at the theater where we're scheduled to perform, stagehands in the employ of the theater will unload it. Crates containing illusions will be unpacked; props will be assembled; costume trunks with pull-out rods will be placed near the wings for quick changes; scenery, backdrops, curtains, and lights will be hung; and the animals will be introduced to their new temporary home. If the show is playing here for a week or more, the animals and people can settle in. If it's a one-night stand, everything will have to be packed up, loaded on trucks and hauled to the train again, so it can be moved to the next town for setup the following day.

If you stop to think about it, the whole thing seems like a daunting and impossible task. But this is the day-to-day routine of a touring illusion show.

The first time I boarded the train as a cast member of the Blackstone show was in October 1947. From town to town and with each successful performance, I felt more and more like a real trouper. Fred Phillips was as good as his word; he was always there to help me through the intricacies of our fast-paced magic show and my new life on the road. Millie Bouton, Pete's wife and our wardrobe mistress, took me under her wing. Everyone in the company was friendly and welcoming. I was "learning the ropes." I felt like I belonged.

I learned my way around the theaters. There were some differences from one to another, but most theaters had dressing rooms on two levels. The downstairs dressing rooms were for company members like me. The animals for the show were kept downstairs, too, where they were fed, watered, and groomed for every performance. The dressing rooms at stage level were for stars like Blackstone.

I was introduced to a whole new lingo. Magicians, and the people who work closely with them, talk in a kind of code that

Jo Abes, Adele, Merle Norton, Sara Graves and Mae Gallagher pose with Blackstone for "Down on the Farm." Publicity photo, 1948.

can sound like gibberish even to other folks in show business. In the backstage lingo of magic, I was a "box jumper" — an assistant who magically appears by jumping out of empty cabinets, or who jumps into boxes only to vanish a moment later.

Not everyone can be a box jumper. There are specific practical requirements for the job, which is why the role is usually performed by young women. Box jumpers for the Blackstone show had to be tiny in stature. Our weight could not exceed 100 pounds. We had to be agile, flexible, and quick, capable of hiding in cramped spaces for an extended time without feeling claustrophobic. We needed good hearing, so we could listen for our cues while tucked away inside illusion boxes. When we

Adele (at left) and Lynn Perry are loaded into an illusion. Nick Ruggiero steadies the box.

made our sudden magical appearances, we had to jump out with bouncy energy and excitement, bow gracefully, then run offstage. The ability to dash about and spin around in high heels was a necessary skill. My dance experience certainly helped.

It's a trick in itself for one girl to squeeze into an illusion cabinet. But sometimes there were two, three, four, or five of us involved in a single illusion. This required much practice and rehearsal, because we had to bunch together in a confined space while taking care not to jostle or elbow one another. Inside the illusion, we had to remain perfectly still, always alert for our cues. The timing had to be perfect. We were all depending on one another. If one person muddled the timing, even by a few seconds, the rest of us would be off, too.

In the big finale of the Blackstone show, we actually had five girls magically appear from two "empty" boxes. While Blackstone was onstage, working "in one" — that is, in front of the main curtain — doing card tricks, rope escapes, and demonstrations of pickpocketing for volunteers from the audience, we box jumpers stood directly behind the curtain, waiting until the last possible moment to conceal ourselves. When the "Committee from the Audience" segment was drawing to a close, into the illusion we went.

I was Number Four of the five girls who would jump out of the boxes, so I was the second to squeeze into our hiding place, where I would lie flat on my back next to Betty Stolle, the fifth and final jumper. With the girls inside and ready to go, the curtains opened for the finale.

Blackstone's "patter" or onstage script was what let us know how many seconds we had before it was time to appear. He used the same words in every show. We would listen for certain words and phrases; when they were spoken, we knew it was our cue to be ready to jump. Some of the illusions were performed to music. During these, Blackstone didn't speak, so we listened for certain notes or phrases in the music and those were our cues. That's why Patty Rose had hummed the music for me when we rehearsed on that first night, before she left the show.

When my cue arrived, three of the girls were already out of the boxes and onstage. I had to do a "crossover," moving from inside one box to the other while remaining hidden from the audience, so the boxes could be opened one at a time and shown empty. When I was in place and ready to appear, I signaled my okay by moving my hands up and down through some slats in the box, a signal that went unseen by the audience. Then, Blackstone and the male assistants unlatched the box and opened it — and there I was!

The male assistants — Frank Gallagher, Harry Rosenberg, and others — were an indispensable part of the performance.

When the boys weren't costumed for a special role, they were dressed as bellhops, as if they were the staff at a posh hotel. Not only did they add a handsome gloss to the show, they would stand by the illusion cabinets, smiling and looking innocent but secretly communicating with the girls who were hiding inside, making sure we were set. After we appeared from inside a box, the boys grasped our arms, lifted us out, and placed us on the stage in one fluid motion. I don't know how they did it, but there were times when they lifted me out and made it look like I was flying.

Membership in the Grand and Glorious Guild of Box Jumpers did not come without a price. In our corps of assistants, there were more than a few men and women who liked to play pranks. Since I was the newcomer, the pranksters decided it was my turn to be initiated into the showbiz fold.

My initiation took place a few days after I joined the company in Philadelphia, while I was still getting to know everyone and adjusting to how quickly my life had changed. The curtain had just come down on that night's magic show and, to my delight, I was asked to join a group going out on the town. "If we hurry," they said, "we can catch the midnight show at the Troc."

The Troc was a Philadelphia theater called The Trocadero. But no one referred to it by its full name; it was always "the Troc." I had done some dance work at several theaters in the city, but the Troc wasn't one of them. Going there would be a new experience. And I didn't realize *how* new.

At the Troc, we passed lobby pictures of showgirls in feathery see-through costumes. *Hmm.* We took two rows of seats, one behind the other. I was starting to get nervous. I had worked with dancers who wore scanty costumes, and comedians who told off-color jokes, and even a few female impersonators who insisted on using the girls' dressing room, but I had never seen what my dear colleagues had brought me to see now: a genuine burlesque show.

Tall, curvy showgirls came out, dancing and prancing around the stage. The comedians "worked blue," as showbiz folks used to say, meaning that the jokes were more than off-color, they were decidedly raunchy. The small group of musicians who comprised the house band pitched in enthusiastically. During comedy skits featuring half-naked girls, the "rip" by the drummer after every punch line made the corny gags, I must say, hilarious. A rousing Sophie Tucker tune by the female piano player provided what the abundantly endowed singer assured us were "authentic songs of the Old West." And then came the main attraction — the strippers, one after the other. These girls were ambitious, stirring the audience with incredible gyrations, while the band's raucous rhythms accompanied every bump and grind.

The people in our group were watching me, waiting to see how I would react. I wasn't exactly shocked by the nudity and crude jokes, but I was also young and seeing a racy show for the first time. My face turned bright scarlet. I thought, *I will concentrate on the costumes.* And truly, the variety was endless: feathers, balloons, ribbons, wisps of cotton, sequins, silks, tassels, gloves — and even fig leaves! Of course, eventually, everything came off, including the leaves. The only things left were the high-heeled shoes on their feet. I thought, *The next thing they'll do is take off their shoes.* Sure enough, in the next scene, all the girls were barefoot and wearing Indian costumes, and these too went the way of everything else. Nothing was left to the imagination.

The strippers went over with wild success, thanks in part to the band's ability to rouse the crowd (and the strippers!) with an irresistible beat. By the end of it, the whole audience was on their feet — yes, including me — shouting, applauding, and yelling for more.

On the way out of the Troc, my showmates laughed and hugged

me. I had met with their approval. They had found out what they wanted to know: I was, in their words, "a good sport" and fit to handle the rough spots in the road ahead.

After Philadelphia, we did shows in Trenton, Newark, and a few other New Jersey towns. We played the DuPont Theatre in Wilmington, Delaware. Then we headed back through Pennsylvania, where we filled bookings in Reading, Allentown, Scranton, Lancaster, Harrisburg, Hershey, Altoona, and Pittsburgh. I was happily sending home two-thirds of my weekly pay, and I still had plenty of paydays in front of me. We were scheduled to tour through the Midwest, with shows in Ohio, Missouri, Wisconsin, and Minnesota.

Between performances, I kept up my dance skills. With Fred's permission, I would run through my dance routines on the empty stage of whatever theater in which we happened to be performing, with just a single work light on the stage. Sometimes, Fred or some of the other company members watched me, and they even applauded as I took my bows to the empty house. Their encouragement warmed my heart. Did Blackstone know about my impromptu dance recitals? I hoped so.

We played to full houses in Ohio. In Youngstown, the show was a great success, as it always had been. But something was wrong with Blackstone. After the show, he had Herbie Washburn, his valet at the time, take him to the hospital. It was an outpatient visit. Blackstone and Herbie then drove to meet us in Akron, where we played the Colonial Theatre on November 10 and 11. Our next engagement was supposed to be a week of shows at the American Theatre in St. Louis. But the cast was notified of the sad news that Blackstone was too ill to perform.

Less than two months after I'd joined the company, the juggernaut that was the Blackstone show came to a sudden and unexpected halt.

3 · OHIO, 1947

Others might have seen it coming. I didn't. To me, it seemed like nothing could stop us. Full houses had been the norm everywhere. Theaters were usually sold out by the time we got there. World War II had only recently come to an end, and millions of men — those lucky enough to have survived — were back with their families. After the privations and separations of wartime, the prevailing mood was one of wanting to cut loose and have a good time. Goodbye *Boogie-Woogie Bugle Boy*, hello *Don't Fence Me In*. The Blackstone show was doing the biggest business in its history, which made what was to come all the more unfortunate.

The first month-and-a-half of my newfound career flew by in a flash. In November, I celebrated my eighteenth birthday — or, more accurately, *we* celebrated. I was treated to a backstage surprise party, complete with "Happy Birthday" sung more or less on key. Stage manager Fred Phillips, smiling from ear to ear, brought out a cake with eighteen blazing candles. And to top off the surprise, a small box wrapped with a ribbon was handed to me by the Boss himself, Harry Blackstone. The busy star of our company had gone out shopping and bought a gift for me. It was an exquisite brooch with pink, blue, and clear stones in the

Adele and The Boss, in the wings, waiting for the curtain to rise.

shape of a ballerina. So he *had* heard about my dancing! (By the way, I still have the brooch. I wear it everywhere and it never fails to get compliments.)

As I opened my birthday gift, Blackstone wished me many more happy years. What I didn't know then was that this master of magic, a man who commanded the forces of nature while onstage, was having trouble breathing.

There was nothing in Blackstone's manner that conveyed how ill he was. He suffered from severe asthma, and the attacks were becoming more and more frequent and debilitating. But there was no understudy for the star of the Blackstone show. The public paid to see *him*. He was accustomed to performing in every circumstance of pain, weariness, and ordinary sickness.

The audiences to whom Blackstone's name was synonymous with magic had no idea that he was struggling to carry on.

It didn't help that he rarely rested. Our schedule called for ten shows a week, a performance every night, with matinees on Wednesdays, Saturdays and Sundays. After the last show of the evening, he would often meet with local magic groups. He loved magic in any form, and in every city to which we traveled there were magic aficionados who were eager to meet him and spend time with him. Dinners were held in his honor. Informal get-togethers were arranged. Shop talk went on into the wee hours of the morning. Blackstone just couldn't say no to these late-night expeditions — until he reached the point that he *had* to. The show demanded all of his energy.

To tell the truth, I saw little of Mr. B other than in the theater and onstage. I didn't know the man well enough to realize his condition. But there were people in the company who knew. They kept a close eye on his health, made sure he took his medication, and encouraged him to get some rest.

Nevertheless, Blackstone's stamina was faltering. Finally, during one of our shows and to the great concern of everyone on and offstage, he seemed to slip into a haze, almost as if he were drunk — which was impossible because he never drank. What was actually happening was that he was being starved of oxygen.

The signal was given to close the curtain. Mr. B wanted to go on, but he couldn't. A public announcement was made that our performances would have to be postponed. The implication was that the show dates would be rescheduled and the tour would be resumed. Backstage, we got the unvarnished truth. Fred Phillips called us all together and gave us the bad news. Blackstone was simply too stricken to continue. The tour would end right here, in Akron, Ohio.

We received our final pay, along with travel expenses for the journey home. I watched in a daze as the illusion cabinets, theatrical equipment, wardrobe trunks, stage hangings, and everything else was crated and bagged for the freight train to Blackstone's headquarters in Colon, Michigan. That's where some of my showmates would be going, too.

Me? I took the train to Philadelphia, back to my parents' house and my work as a solo dance act.

4 · BORN *to* DANCE

I was born in Philadelphia in the winter of 1929, and by the time I was twelve years old I was serious about dancing. I'd started taking dance classes at the Sherwood Recreation Center when I was nine. The classes were free, and they were taught by a young lady named Helen Clavan. To me, even in the humble surroundings of the recreation center, Miss Clavan seemed glamorous. She taught me the basics of tap and ballet. I practiced at home and couldn't wait for the next class. A few years later, she opened her own dance studio just a few blocks from our house. My family couldn't afford to pay for weekly dance lessons at the studio. Miss Clavan suggested that I could "earn a scholarship" by cleaning the dance studio every day after school. She knew how much those classes meant to me. I swept the floors, kept the waiting room neat, cleared shoes and bags from the benches, and cleaned the huge mirrors that covered the wall behind the ballet bar. And my studies continued.

Three weeks after my twelfth birthday, Japan attacked Pearl Harbor, and the United States went to war. My dad felt it was his duty to reenlist in the Navy. Early in 1942, he shipped out to England and then to France. Two years later, he was sent to the South Pacific. I was the oldest of four children, so I became responsible for some of the jobs that had been my father's: stoking the fire in our coal stove, shoveling ashes into a large container for trash day, helping my siblings with their homework. I also did a lot of the cooking. My chores included going to the Acme store butcher to get free kidneys for stew, and beef heart, which we kids thought was steak. I always asked for a soup bone and bought day-old bread for one penny a loaf. In straight language, we were downright poor. We even depended on neighbors' hand-me-downs for clothing.

At home, my mother was *the boss*. While my father was away, she made all the decisions. Just before I entered high school, she made a big decision for me. She enrolled me at her alma mater, the hospital nursing school, so I could follow in her footsteps and become a registered nurse. This turned out to be very stressful. I fainted at the sight of blood. I shuddered when a doctor or nurse headed in my direction with a needle. A career in nursing was not my idea of a happy future, but I had to obey my mother. So I tried. I took chemistry courses and studied Latin. Fortunately, she let me continue my dance lessons.

I was thirteen when Miss Clavan married Dr. Nathan Reese, a dentist. When they became parents of a little boy, I was asked to babysit so they could enjoy an occasional evening out. Their son Merrill loved to be entertained; I loved being silly and making him giggle. Today, Merrill Reese is famous as the voice of the Philadelphia Eagles football team, reporting play-by-play action for radio-listening Eagles fans.

Helen Clavan Reese encouraged me to pursue my dance training. She recommended I study with a husband-and-wife dance team who had a studio nearby.

Sid Gray and Madeleine Arden were professional dance partners. He was a good tap teacher and she had a fine background in ballet. But what they taught wasn't just about dance; it was about being a dancer. They taught me the ins and outs of show business, how to be a polished performer, how to "sell" a dance routine and turn it into a real act. By the time I was sixteen and a junior in high school, they'd given me the confidence to begin looking for paying jobs. They recommended theatrical agents for me to contact in Philadelphia, and those agents gave me my first contracts. Soon enough, I was working as a dancer in theaters and nightclubs, at club dates and conventions, and on the stages of hotels and inns.

One summer, I worked a few weeks at a sideshow on Hamid's Pier in Atlantic City, New Jersey. I was a dancer on the tiny stage in front of the tent, enticing people to buy a ticket for the show. Inside, folks passed an exhibit of strange creatures floating in jars. When the show started, they were introduced to the world's tallest man, the world's smallest man, the world's fattest woman, and a lady who looked like a gorilla. I did my song-and-dance routine to the sounds of a three-piece combo.

During my senior year in high school, I received a scholarship for three months of Saturday ballet classes with Madame LeSylphe at the Roseland Building in New York. I traveled alone by train and bus. Those lessons really paid off. My toe dancing became refined and my act took on a Broadway style, which was good for bookings.

I didn't have a car or even a license to drive, so I had to depend on my mother to get me to the places where I worked. I was the opening act, usually doing two numbers. After the singers, comedians, jugglers, magicians and other variety acts performed, I did two more dance numbers to close the show. My mother would sit in the dressing room or take a seat near the stage entrance during the performance. I know she enjoyed meeting and talking with the other performers wherever we went.

As graduation approached, I was very concerned that my mother would tell me I had to stop my dance career. Even though my dad was home from the war, he did not overrule my mother's

Publicity photo for Adele Friel, Song & Dance Nightclub act, "That Old Black Magic," 1946.

decisions. So, I was happy and relieved when she agreed to let me dance. By then, with agents keeping me busy with bookings on Fridays and Saturdays — the city didn't permit Sunday shows in nightclubs back then — and with my part-time job after school as a salesperson at Sears & Roebuck, I was earning a steady income for the family.

Each of my dance routines required specially arranged sheet music for the band to play. I was lucky to get the best music arranger in Philadelphia: Evans Brown. I met Evans when I was working in the chorus line at Palumbo's in South Philadelphia. He was an old-time rehearsal pianist, and he specialized in arranging music to match the personality of the performer. Evans usually conducted his meetings outside the Shubert Theatre on Broad Street, where many theatrical agents had their offices. He was a chain-smoker, always with a cigarette dangling from his lips, always surrounded by a cloud of smoke. But nobody cared, because he was great at what he did. He put together excellent sheet music, whether it was for a full band or a small combo.

After I graduated from high school, I had more time to devote to my dance career. In those days, my act featured one of my favorite dance numbers. I wore a black two-piece costume with sheer sleeves and black toe shoes. The music I chose was a song by Harold Arlen and Johnny Mercer: "That Old Black Magic." That was several months before I met or had even heard of Harry Blackstone. Funny how things work out that way.

5 · Picture Postcard

It bore a green one-cent stamp. The front showed a black-and-white photo of Harry Blackstone's lakeside home in Colon, Michigan. On the reverse side was a message addressed to me, written in Blackstone's hand, and dated December 16, 1947:

> *Hi ya!*
> *Thanks a lot for all the pleasant thots am feeling a lot better.*
> *A good rest is all I need now.*
> *Merry Xmas*
> *Harry B*

6 · THE ELUSIVE MOTH

1947 became 1948. Soon, the colors of springtime transformed the city, as if by magic. Time and again, my thoughts returned to the Blackstone show. *Will it ever go on the road again? And if it does, will I be in it?*

When the answers to those questions finally arrived, I could hardly believe my luck. I received two hand-written letters from Harry Blackstone. The first explained that he was creating a new illusion called the Elusive Moth — and he wanted me to star in it! The second letter provided a few details about how the illusion would be staged, including some ideas about a special costume. Costume fittings and rehearsals for this new illusion would require my presence in Michigan. How soon could I be there?

How soon is right now?

It took me about three days to get my trunk packed, notify my theatrical agents that I would be leaving town, purchase a one-way ticket, and board an overnight train bound for Battle Creek, Michigan. Fred Phillips met me at the station. He'd been summering in one of the small cabins on the Blackstone property, where folks were getting things ready for the upcoming tour.

Fred drove us the 33 miles south to Colon, Michigan. The little village seemed to be dozing in the summer sun. It was exactly the kind of refuge that a traveling showman would choose if he were looking for a spot off the beaten path, far from the crowds, the razzle-dazzle, and the rigors of the road.

At the Blackstone homestead, no one was dozing. When I arrived, Pete Bouton, Mr. B, and several assistants were working in the famous red barn, the creative workshop where new illusions were hatched. Blackstone looked hale and hearty, totally recovered from the ordeal in Ohio. I was ready to pitch in and paint an illusion cabinet or two, but fourteen-year-old Harry Jr. had other ideas. He wanted me to help him paint his canoe, so we'd be able paddle it out on Sturgeon Lake. Harry Jr. won the day. We painted the canoe blue.

Later on, Mr. B described his vision for the Elusive Moth. I would play the title role, a moth caught in a spider's web. The moth struggles to free herself as she is hoisted up above the stage. Putting some distance between me and the stage floor would eliminate suspicion of trap doors. With a puff of smoke, the moth disappears in midair. Blackstone pictured this as a fast-moving dramatic sketch, set in a jungle, with a howling savage tribe as my pursuers and captors. All my dance practice on empty stages was about to pay off. I was being cast as the lead in a featured illusion. This was my big chance to show how vivid and artistic I could make it.

Walter Gibson arrived at Blackstone Island. Walter was Harry Blackstone's best friend. He was also Blackstone's ghost writer and chronicler. When souvenir programs had to be written or when news items were submitted to the papers, Walter wrote them. Before I joined the show, Walter had toured with Blackstone for a year, writing reports about the great magician for every newspaper and radio station wherever they went. He was the perfect man for the task. Not only was Walter Gibson a talented magician, he was the author who had created Lamont Cranston and his crime-fighting alter ego, The Shadow, the title character of the popular radio serial. For a time, the voice of The Shadow was provided by a magician named Orson Welles. Joining a magic show taught me that magic and magicians are everywhere.

Blackstone didn't drive, so when he had an appointment in a nearby town or city, Walter Gibson was usually the man behind the wheel. And that's exactly where he was, in the driver's seat, on our trip to Chicago for an appointment at Lanquay Costumers. I sat in the back, feeling nervous about being measured and fitted for my Elusive Moth costume. In the front, Walter and Mr. B chatted casually about new tricks for the show, the places we would visit on the upcoming tour, the need to find a couple of new assistants for the cast, and the practical question of where we would have lunch after our meeting with the costume designer.

The designer, Guy Moore, was waiting for us. He had already sketched out his plans for the costume. The three of us examined the drawings and the materials he had chosen. It was important for the costume to be dramatic and eye-catching, but also durable and easy to wear, requiring no ironing and allowing a full range of motion. All of these demands were met. My nervousness began to vanish as I was caught up in the excitement of imagining what the audience would see: the spider web, the moth, the savage pursuers, the puff of smoke...

I stood as still as I could for the costume fitting. A tape measure, a pencil for jotting down notes, a few pins, and a big smile were the tools Guy Moore used to get the job done. In a short time, I was wearing a muslin model of the costume. The final fitting would take place on a return trip to Chicago, and on that day we would bring the finished costume back to Blackstone headquarters. The sewing schedule for the construction of the costume was pushed to the limit, because the show had to be on the road in a matter of weeks.

Lon Ramsdell did the driving for that second trip to Chicago

Studio photo with Blacksone, company members, and the Elusive Moth.

with Mr. B and me. Harry Jr. was with us, too. We were there to pick up three costumes: the Elusive Moth and two outfits that I'd wear for the Costume Trunk illusion. I couldn't wait to see them! As it turned out, I had to contain my excitement for another day, because the costumes weren't quite ready. More time was needed to put on the finishing touches. So, we checked into a hotel and stayed overnight in the Windy City. The next day, we picked up three beautiful costumes made especially for me. The grand total for all three was $247.

A great deal of handwork went into the finished Elusive Moth costume, making it a unique piece of art. It was a three-piece costume. The top, bottom, and headpiece were made of a satiny material, mostly in shades of green, with dashes of orange, purple, dark red, and black accents. The headgear was close-fitting, like a swimmer's cap, with a strap that snapped under my chin. My hair was hidden, but my face was visible. Two colorful "eyes" were prominent just above my own eyes. On the top of the cap was a fanciful "antenna." The bottom and top of the costume were formfitting without restricting my ability to move. Long sleeves were attached at the shoulders, and a neckband decorated the neckline.

And, of course, a moth must have wings. My wings were spectacular. Multicolored expanses of gossamer silk were attached to the top part of the costume, and I held a silk-covered 24-inch dowel in each hand, which extended my wingspan well beyond my outstretched arms. When I wore my toe shoes and stood on point, the bottom tips of the wings just barely touched the stage, and the material fluttered and waved as I danced and twirled.

The savage pursuers wore animal-print costumes and frightening masks, with carved red lips, menacing eyes and eyebrows, and matted hair. The Moth was chased across the stage and forced toward the giant spider web. I tried to escape by leaping and spinning, but I was captured and rolled up in the web. My wings fluttered helplessly as the web was hoisted up into the air. Just when the situation seemed hopeless, Blackstone saved the day: with a magical gesture, he conjured a sudden burst of smoke. When the smoke cleared, my captors gazed in amazement as the web unraveled. It was empty. The Moth, now truly elusive, was gone.

Del Ray played the Witch Doctor for the scene. His costume had extra jewelry to indicate his importance. Tom Reid played the Jungle Chief. His costume had the most feathers.

The Elusive Moth poses with two "jungle natives," Harry Rosenberg and Del Ray.

With all the costumes and props ready, we rehearsed the action. The back area of the red barn was converted into a rehearsal stage; if necessary, changes to the illusion could be made right there in the workshop. Blackstone wanted nothing slow or long-winded in his show. As we ran through the scene, we kept speeding up the pace. Rough spots were smoothed out. Sometimes it took too long for me to be caught in the web. Sometimes the wild tribe wasn't wild enough. A few times, the smoke cloud was triggered too early or too late. Eventually, everything was the way the Boss wanted it. The Elusive Moth, along with the rest of this monumental show, was ready to hit the road.

August 18, 1948, at the Erlanger Theatre in Chicago — the first performance of the Elusive Moth in front of an audience. What

The Moth and Native (Nick Ruggiero) pose backstage. Early 1949.

an unforgettable thrill that was! There were gasps of surprise when the Moth vanished, and sustained applause at the end of the scene. It was such a delight to us and a real tribute to Blackstone's sense of theater. The Elusive Moth was a hit.

In many ways, I think that illusion epitomized everything the Blackstone show had to offer: magic and mystery, action, excitement, spectacle, beauty — and even humor, in the baffled way the tribe reacted to the loss of its sacrificial captive.

Every performance of the Elusive Moth went off without a hitch, from the audience's point of view. But there was one instance when something went wrong *after* the illusion. On that occasion, as the audience applauded, Blackstone turned away from the empty net in which the Moth had been held prisoner until her sudden disappearance, the curtain closed, and the

Adele Friel Rhindress | 35

master magician began his next trick. A stagehand missed his cue and forgot to release me from the other net, the *real* net, in which I was still a prisoner. I was too tangled up to move, trapped on my back, suspended above the stage. I couldn't make a sound or call for help, because Blackstone was performing just a few feet away from where I was dangling, helpless and trying not to panic.

Millie, our wardrobe mistress, realized that I was missing when I didn't show up for my next costume change. She found a stagehand to operate the ropes and lower the net to the stage floor, where they could quietly untangle me. Blackstone never found out that, for a while, his Elusive Moth really *had* disappeared.

I believe I am the only person who ever played the Elusive Moth. I'm told that my costume is in David Copperfield's vast collection of magic props and memorabilia.

The combined efforts of many people, onstage and offstage, were required to perform the wonders in the Blackstone show. Nevertheless, even though no one else ever danced the dance of the Elusive Moth, and as proud as I am of the work I did in the show, I have to admit that I was replaceable.

Blackstone was irreplaceable. It was his name and stage presence that sold the tickets. As we'd seen in Ohio, the show couldn't go on without its star. But I can think of another person without whom the Blackstone tour would have come to an immediate stop.

7 · Pete *and* Millie Bouton

Actually, I should have said *two* people, because they were a matched set, husband and wife: Pete and Millie Bouton. The Blackstone show had begun as a double act. Brothers Harry and Pete were born with the name Boughton, but they changed it to Bouton when they first went on the road as a magic-and-comedy duo. Harry eventually became Blackstone, the visible star of the show. Pete kept the name Bouton and became the wizard behind the scenes. But from a certain point of view, the Blackstone show remained a double act. Each brother had to rely on the other's abilities. Harry called Pete "the mainspring of my watch" and, as far as I could see, that was absolutely true. The show as I knew it could not have gone on without Pete.

Onstage, Blackstone commanded the attention and interest of the audience. Backstage, Pete Bouton was in command. He was our "everything" man, responsible for every piece of physical equipment in the show.

When we were on the road, Pete made sure that all the orange-painted crates, along with his fire-engine red workshop on wheels, were transported from the train and loaded into the theater. The load-in process was an amazing study in precision, a kind of ballet in which a misstep could have disastrous results.

When the equipment arrived at the stage dock, Pete directed each crate to a specific place at the backstage wall. These spots were reserved for the large equipment, the big illusions. Smaller tricks went to other locations along the sides of the backstage area. A special crate housed the electric organ, our only traveling musical instrument, the backbone for local musicians who joined our show in various cities. The organ was set up in the orchestra pit or on the floor in front of the stage.

Pete kept everything in proper working order. If a prop or illusion needed to be repaired, his portable workshop was at the ready. Before the curtain went up, Pete and assistants Del Ray and Nick Ruggiero inspected every illusion and prop. Everything, down to the last silk handkerchief, was checked to make sure it was set for the show. Electrical connections had to be hooked up for the Buzz Saw illusion. The glass had to be spotless for the Crystal Casket. The spider web had to be hung for the Elusive Moth. Flash pots had to be set. Sheet music had to be in the correct order.

Pete and Millie pose backstage. In front of them is the bar on which Millie hung the girls' wardrobe.

During the show, Pete monitored every trick from start to finish, making sure everything went smoothly, staying alert in case something unexpected happened. He was the most trusted and valuable man behind the scenes, every step of the way.

When it was time to move the show to the next city, Pete

Pete (at left) orchestrated every backstage moment and movement of the show.

supervised the process of loading out all of the equipment. He saw to it that everything was disassembled and packed correctly, loaded on the trucks, hauled to the train, and transferred to the freight cars. Choreographing this process again and again, ensuring that nothing was lost or broken, required remarkable skills.

Pete and I got along well right from the start, and he became a father-by-proxy to me. Stagehands often asked me out for dinner or a date, and Pete was always right there to give me the okay or not. I was a young girl away from home for the first time, and he figured I should be looked after. There was nothing stern or stiff-necked about this. I can still see Pete's lively eyes and friendly face. He was a mellow soul. He had traveled the nation for years;

Adele Friel Rhindress | 39

he knew all the theaters and the men who worked in them. He was on an amiable "How's the family?" basis with practically everyone, everywhere we went.

I trusted Pete implicitly. He could be imposing in his job when he had to be, but he was a kindhearted person with a veteran trouper's understanding of human nature. When he told me never to go out with the "Stage-door Johnnies" who were always waiting to invite the girls to dinner or a drink after the show, I had the good sense to realize that Pete knew what he was talking about. I didn't go out for drinks, because I didn't drink. And I never did go out with any Stage-door Johnnies.

Among the trucks that hauled the equipment for the show was one that carried the all-important wardrobe trunks. Pete's wife, Millie, was in charge of those. Millie was short in stature, barely five feet tall with her shoes on, and was always ready with a smile. Even though her brown hair was short and styled in neat waves close to her head, she wore her little black hat. I thought of it as her miniature top hat, with its off-white plume attached to the left side, cascading down to meet her ear.

As wardrobe mistress, Millie was present at load-in, pointing out where the many wardrobe trunks should go. She made sure every trunk was properly positioned at stage left or stage right, depending on where each of us would make entrances and exits. She opened the trunks, set up the racks, and unpacked the costumes, hanging each garment in the exact order in which it would be used.

In the Blackstone show, every illusion, trick, or walk-on was accompanied by a change of costume. Each of the six girl assistants had fifteen costume changes during the show. If one of the girls was feeling sick and was unable to perform, a few of us would divvy up her scenes and stand in for her. On those occasions, we might have 23 costume changes. Many of these were

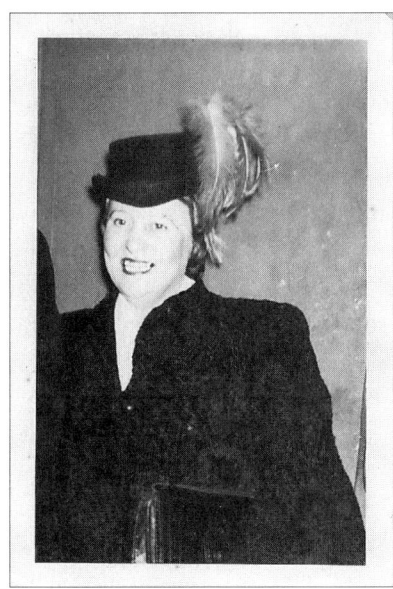

Millie at night's end, ready for a post-performance meal.

fast changes, completed in a minute or less. Even with Millie there to help us, there was no time to run to a dressing room, so most of the costume changes took place in the wings, at the sides of the stage, partially screened by the wardrobe trunks. The only "permanent" items of clothing we wore were our high-heeled silver shoes and underpants. The rest of our costumes were flung on and off as necessary. This presented plenty of temptation for backstage Peeping Toms. However, as every stagehand learned, Millie was a tigress when it came to protecting *her girls*. In every city and town, she laid down the law: there would be no gawking from up in the flies or anywhere else. I sometimes watched and listened as she delivered this warning, enjoying every minute of it. Millie, a five-foot-high force of nature, made it very clear that she was to be taken seriously and wouldn't tolerate any shenanigans. It worked.

In every theater we played, Millie had her own wardrobe room, which was filled with costumes — some waiting for a stitch or two, others ready to be sent to the cleaners for the fastest possible service before the show that night. There was a sewing machine, an iron and ironing board, and a row of containers filled with spools of colored thread, sequins, feathers, ribbons, zippers, glue, scissors, safety pins, and even some Band-Aids.

I wanted to get acquainted with Millie, beyond just relying on her as our wardrobe mistress. Millie knew the ropes. She was aware of everything that went on backstage and offstage, and she could offer valuable insight. So one day, I stopped by her wardrobe room. Millie was busy ironing a gown for the opening act. I offered to help her if she had an extra task that needed to be done. She asked "Can you sew?" I said yes. "Then follow me," she said. We went out onto the stage and behind a backdrop curtain. She moved a brightly colored cabinet away from the wall, opened the door, and pulled out a mummy. It was a prop mummy, of course, one that Blackstone danced with in the first act. Its white bandages had become loose and frayed. "It needs a tummy-tuck" was how Millie described the sewing chore to which I was assigned.

Back in the wardrobe room, Dr. Adele took needle, thread, and thimble and performed a two-hour surgery on the ancient Egyptian. I have to say that I did a good job of it. While we worked, Millie and I chatted back and forth. We talked about costumes, the show, and her life on the road with Pete. They'd been married in a lakeside ceremony at Blackstone Island in the summer of 1935 and they were very devoted to each other. She had a positive attitude about traveling from place to place and living out of a trunk, but she also said how much she enjoyed the off months, when she could spend time at her home in Colon, Michigan. Millie was not a fan of Mr. B and she wasn't shy about expressing her opinion. She put up with him, she said, "for Pete's sake."

Those two hours of conversation blossomed into a warm friendship. I was always welcome in the wardrobe room. And that night, Harry Blackstone danced with the best-dressed mummy in town.

8 · SEX *and* SO FORTH

Fred Phillips was a superb stage manager, an invaluable personal assistant to Harry Blackstone, and a good friend to me. Fred and I had many lunches and dinners together and lots of interesting conversations. Fred's hometown was St. Louis, Missouri. When we played the American Theatre there in October 1948, he introduced me to his mother, sister, and aunt. He told me that he had been married and was the father of an eight-year-old daughter, Judy. After World War II, the marriage ended in divorce. He'd discovered that his wife had been unfaithful. His ex-wife took their child to Cuba and then to South America. I don't know if he ever saw them again. Being a member of the Blackstone company gave Fred a focus that helped him cope and move on with his life.

Fred was gay. In those days, it was not unusual for gay men to forsake what would make them happy in life and to instead do what was expected of a man: marry a woman and start a family. Fred's traveling magic-show family knew about his preferences, and we respected him as a goodhearted person and a fine leader in his managerial role.

When I met him, Fred was in his early thirties, a blue-eyed blond with an easygoing smile that flashed a gold tooth. He had

Adele and Fred costumed for the "Chinese Fantasy" routine.

a great sense of humor, but when show time arrived there was no goofing around. He went into action and demanded that everyone toe the line. From his many years of trouping, Fred could point us toward his favorite restaurants and hotels in all the towns where we played. He was always the first to arrive at the theater, and among the last to leave. He was a kind and considerate soul, and his generosity, upbeat spirit, and sunny outlook helped to set the tone for the whole company.

In addition to being our stage manager, Fred acted as a valet to Mr. Blackstone. He made sure that Mr. B's wardrobe trunk was placed and opened in the star's dressing room, and that Blackstone's white-tie-and-tails were always immaculate — evening clothes and backups freshly dry-cleaned and pressed;

Fred, Adele, and Trixie pose with the cannon for the Sepoy Mutiny illusion.

formal shirts laundered, starched, and spotlessly white; black shoes shined to a high gloss. Blackstone never had to search around for his stage make-up; Fred made sure it was all laid out. And in case the great magician wanted to stretch out and relax during a rare moment of downtime, Fred saw to it that there was a cot in the dressing room, along with anything else that could make the place more comfortable.

As stage manager, Fred ran the show. It was his job to make sure that everyone was ready to go at show time. When the curtain went up, he was responsible for everything that happened onstage and backstage until after the final curtain call, when all the magic props were stored, all the costumes replaced on the racks, all the animals secured, all the personnel on their way to late meals, and Blackstone himself was probably in a cab headed toward a magic club.

Back then, every cue for every curtain, lighting change, scene change, and flash pot was run manually. And then there were all of the props and illusions that had to be placed onstage and taken offstage. In the midst of coordinating all this activity, Fred also donned a costume and acted as an assistant during some of the routines. He was one of the savage tribesmen in the Elusive Moth, and he was the "boy" who climbed the rope and vanished in the Hindu Rope Mystery. He also appeared in the opening scene, the Enchanted Garden. This was a full-stage tableau that dazzled the audience with spectacular magic and lavish costumes. The scene was set in Colonial times. When the curtain opened, the entire cast was posed onstage, the girls in pastel gowns and tall white wigs, the boys in powdered wigs, pastel waistcoats, knee-breeches, long white hose, black silver-buckled shoes, and silky shirts with high collars.

Those high collars looked mighty nice onstage, but they tended to pick up greasepaint from the face and neck. In an effort to make myself useful, I offered to wash Fred's high-collared shirt after the shows, so it would always be neat and greasepaint-free at the start of the day. Fred was delighted. Each night, I took Fred's shirt back to my hotel room and washed it in the sink. The next morning, I pressed it on Millie's happily provided ironing board at the theater.

In time, I took on other tasks for Fred. To obtain some items for the show, we had to contact pet shops and beverage distributors in each town. So, after checking in at the hotel, I immediately grabbed a phone book and looked for pet shops that might have rabbits for sale — small ones. During the show, a bunny would be conjured up for a lucky child in the audience. I made arrangements for the bunnies to be delivered to the theater a few hours before show time. Next, I called the local beverage

Blackstone featured a routine in which he produced bottles of beer. The libations were supplied by local distributors.

distributors and bargained for freebies in exchange for an onstage endorsement from the master magician himself. After audience volunteers assisted in a trick, Mr. B would send them back to their seats with, say, a six-pack of Coca-Cola or Dr. Pepper while giving the product a ringing recommendation. It was basically a live, onstage commercial delivered by Harry Blackstone, and I'm sure it sold plenty of soda.

I'll always remember phoning a livestock dealer in Laredo, Texas, not looking for a bunny but a burro. One night, after the theater was closed, our small horse named Trixie got loose from the enclosure and wandered over to the men's dressing room, where she found some black shoe polish. She ate it. Whatever was in that shoe polish killed her. We were very sad. We were also in a jam, because we didn't have a trained animal to appear from The Drum That Can't Be Beat and to walk across the stage with me in the marketplace scene for the Sepoy Mutiny illusion. But the dealer in Laredo was able to help. Sally the Burro arrived two days later. That night, with no rehearsal at all, she joined the cast of the Blackstone show. And she performed perfectly.

Fred Phillips liked things to be neat and clean and organized, not just in the theater but in his life. Maybe that's one of the reasons why we got along so well. We became good friends, almost like roommates. Whenever possible, Fred booked connecting rooms for us. Sometimes the room had a shared bath in between. Being next door allowed him to keep a protective eye on the youngster of the company and it gave me a comforting sense of security to know that he was close by.

Sometimes, the effort to control the cost of moving a big illusion show from city to city made it necessary for me to have a real roommate, so I had to share a room with a girl in the troupe. One of my regular roommates was Betty Stolle. She was a fun, friendly, down-to-earth person who warmly welcomed me into the magic-show family, even when a few of the girls thought I didn't "fit in." Betty had worked with Blackstone in the USO during World War II, performing magic shows at military bases. Some of those performances took place in the middle of the night, just before the troops left from local airfields for foreign duty. She was an expert magician's assistant and truly the embodiment of what the ads for the show promised when they referred to Blackstone's bevy of "Gorgeous Girls." Betty was featured in the Princess Karnac levitation, the Buzz Saw illusion, the Crystal Casket, the Light Bulb Cabinet, and she appeared in many walk-on moments during the show. After the final curtain, she often accompanied the Boss to dinners and parties thrown by magic clubs in the cities and towns on our tour. Betty dressed to the nines. Her wardrobe trunk bulged with lovely clothes.

It wasn't just the dinners and parties that kept Betty out late

Mr. B surrounded by magnificently costumed company members, advertised as "gorgeous girls." Early 1940s.

or, on occasion, all night. Betty was head-over-heels in love, and her boyfriend's name was Harry Blackstone — Senior. Every day, she told me how much she loved him and that she would gladly give up her plan to pursue a career in acting if only he would pop the question. Their age difference — thirty-plus years — didn't matter to Betty, nor did the fact that he'd been twice married and divorced.

In some people's opinions, Harry Blackstone was a womanizer. I thought of him as a ladies' man, someone who thrived on female attention. One day in the summer of 1948, he was apparently in an amorous mood, and he and I happened to be alone together. It was perfect timing — for him. He took action. It was more than just a wink or a word or a touch. For his age, he was strong. But I got free before anything really serious happened.

I didn't mention that incident to anyone until the day I was reunited with Nick Ruggiero, 54 years after we had been assistants together in the Blackstone show. Nick asked me in the presence of one of my grown sons, "Did Blackstone ever try to romance you?" My son Bob was very surprised by my answer. His words still ring in my ears: "I can't believe the world's greatest magician tried to seduce my mom when she was a teenager!" I assured Bob and Nick that Blackstone didn't win that battle, and I was okay.

My rejection of Blackstone's advances led to a couple of bonuses for me: first, he never tried anything with me again; and second, whenever Harry Junior had a school break and came to visit his famous father, Harry Sr. relied on me to be a friend to his son. I'd get a phone call in the morning, inviting me to join the two of them for breakfast at their hotel. After breakfast, Junior and I would go shopping. At fourteen years of age, Harry Jr. was very tall and, like his father, had a magnificent voice. He usually tried to act grown-up and serious, but even though I was four years older, I think being around another teenager allowed him to let loose and have fun. We always enjoyed hanging out with each other.

And what happened to Betty Stolle? I'm told that she never married and never gave up on the idea that she and Harry Blackstone were meant for each other. To her dying day, she carried the torch for the remarkable magician who had disappeared from her life.

9 · PLACES *and* FACES

Looking back to my time with the Blackstone show, I find that certain people, places, and images stand out in my memory. For instance…

Chicago, Illinois. Mr. B grew up in the Windy City. The cheers and ovations he always received there were, in part, recognition for a hometown boy made good.

We were in Chicago for a three-week run. The theater was located in the Loop, right in the thick of the big-city activity. Elevated trains roared by overhead. Paperboys were hawking the news. Night and day, chaser lights danced around the theater marquee, where the name BLACKSTONE let everyone know that the world's greatest magic show was in town.

Every show was selling out. Mr. B was in good health. The energy he brought to the Enchanted Garden number at the top of the show inspired all of us to give 100 percent. Blackstone was an extraordinary entertainer; for two-and-a-half hours he held the audience under his spell and brought a smile to everyone's face, even us folks in the cast.

The excitement generated during the show was often so great that none of us wanted to go back to the hotel afterward. So instead, we hit the town and celebrated. On one occasion, we all went to a nightclub for their late dinner and stage show. There was a singing emcee, a roller-skating act, a tap dancer, and the headliner was the music-and-comedy trio of Clayton, Jackson, and Durante — Jimmy Durante, that is, with his partners Eddie Jackson and Lou Clayton. Does it get any better than that?

Detroit, Michigan. Leave it to me to get into trouble. It all began when we had one of our rare days off. Some of the cast, mostly the guys, headed to the nearest magic shop to meet people and do card tricks. A few of the girls went shopping for clothes. I found out that *Madame Butterfly* was being performed by the Detroit Opera Company that evening, so I bought a ticket and was seated in the last row of the highest part of the peanut gallery. What a show it was! The voices, the costumes, the scenery — it was all so beautiful, it brought tears to my eyes.

Wednesdays, Saturdays and Sundays were long workdays, with afternoon and evening performances, and we would all be tuckered out by the end of the last show. The day after the opera was one of those long and tiring days, and it was almost midnight when I got back to the hotel. I locked the door, slipped off my shoes, and then I dropped, fully clothed and utterly exhausted, onto the bed.

The next thing I knew, the phone was ringing. It was Fred Phillips. He was shouting, "Del? Where have you been? Are you okay? I just called half-hour! The curtain goes up in 29 minutes!"

I had slept almost twenty hours.

"Don't talk," he said. "Just throw some water on your face and go down to the front door of the hotel. Someone will be waiting to drive you to the theater."

I rushed down to the lobby. A man yelled "Are you Del?" He was a Detroit police officer and he was standing next to the open door of a squad car. I nodded and hopped in. He drove full speed,

From left: Jo Habes, Blackstone, and Adele Friel (age 18). Publicity photo, 1948.

with the lights flashing and the siren blaring. Cars swerved out of the way. He got me there in fifteen minutes.

Fred was waiting with my silver shoes. Millie Bouton got me into the colonial costume and white wig for the opening number. The overture was ending — no time for make-up. I took my place onstage with barely two seconds to spare. Harry Blackstone never found out that I had almost missed the first act.

La Crosse, Wisconsin. I had several hours to spare before the matinee and decided to do some sightseeing. So I set out with a sandwich in my pocket, just in case I got hungry. It was a lovely fall day. The trees were turning bright red and yellow in a park by the widest river I had ever seen. I sat on a park bench, ate my sandwich, and tossed pieces of bread to the late-season birds. After watching the birds peck away for a while, I looked up and saw something I'll never forget: gliding through the water was a magnificent white riverboat with a huge paddlewheel at the back, just like in the movie *Show Boat*. I'd never seen a real riverboat before, and here was the very archetype of one, making its way down the legendary Mississippi. Can you blame me if I broke into a chorus of "Ol' Man River"?

Burlington, Vermont. Our tour schedules were planned well in advance. An unscheduled performance was a rare event. One such occasion was February 20, 1949. We had just completed a week of sold-out shows at His Majesty's Theatre in Montreal, Canada, and were on our way to Newark, New Jersey, where we were scheduled to perform for a week at the Opera House, starting on February 21. Blackstone announced that we'd be making a stop in Burlington, Vermont, so he could repay a favor to a friend. I can't recall who the friend was — it might have been the mayor of Burlington — or what favor was being repaid. The person and the favor must have been important, because it wasn't a simple task to divert the *Show of 1001 Wonders* to a blizzardy town for a one-night stand.

Pete Bouton arranged for trucks to back up to the train siding and pick up every prop, illusion, costume, animal, and even the electric organ, and transport all of it to the local theater. The whole town was buzzing about the show. People were so excited to have the world's most famous magician paying a visit, they went out of their way to help. No one had to hail a cab that day. Folks picked us up in their own cars and drove us to the theater.

We all scrambled to perform the best show we could. It was a packed house, standing room only, at the Kiwanis International

Auditorium. We took no intermission, did a condensed show, and after each illusion and routine was completed, the equipment was loaded back onto the trucks for the return trip to the train station. The evening ended with a standing ovation like no other.

The train was a sleeper, and we were all grateful for the chance to catch forty winks before arriving in New Jersey. We'd worked hard to provide a fun show on that snowy night. Whatever favor the Boss owed had surely been repaid.

St. Louis, Missouri. We were playing St. Louis during the week leading up to the presidential election of 1948. The nation's press, most of it anyway, was predicting a win for Thomas Dewey from New York. Harry Truman, although he was the incumbent president — he'd stepped into office when Franklin Roosevelt died in 1945 — was to some people almost a laughingstock, this little pipsqueak of a guy.

Truman's home was Independence, Missouri, so he was a favorite son to the people of that state. When news came over the radio that Truman had won the election, the city erupted in celebration. Traffic stopped on the streets, and crowds of merrymakers laughed, cried, screamed, set off fireworks and ran around, waving American flags.

The excitement was contagious, especially for Fred Phillips, who had grown up in St. Louis. That night, we all gathered in the hotel lobby. We didn't want to miss any of the fun, so we stayed up all night, talking with people, munching snacks, and waiting for the morning newspaper. When it came, the front page featured the now-famous photo of Truman grinning from ear to ear while holding up a newspaper bearing the headline "DEWEY DEFEATS TRUMAN."

The gala atmosphere that followed the election was great for the Blackstone show. The people of Missouri were in a mood to have fun. Capacity crowds filled the theater for every performance,

Adele poses backstage with a rabbit that would later be given away to a lucky volunteer.

and I can remember the rousing cheers and many curtain calls for *our* Harry, the world's greatest magician.

In a week, I would be having a celebration of my own. It would be my nineteenth birthday.

Boston, Massachusetts. Christmas week — ten sellout shows, with performances every night, and matinees on Wednesday, Saturday and Sunday. The streets were filled with people in brightly colored coats, scarves, and hats. Some of the trees glittered with tiny white Christmas lights. Snowflakes sparkled on paths and benches on the Common.

Harry Junior and I were doing one of our favorite things:

shopping. He was on a school break and, as always, he had taken the opportunity to meet up with the show. We strolled past the stores, admiring the colorful window displays. In one shop, Harry found a nice Christmas gift for his dad.

Having completed the shopping expedition, we cut through the park, where the snow was untouched, pure and white. Harry Junior was fifteen years old. No teenager can walk past a pristine patch of snow without making a snowball. Harry picked up a handful of snow, rolled it into a ball, and lobbed it at me. Of course, I couldn't resist a bit of payback with a snowball of my own. After a brief but vigorous snowball fight, we flopped down on our backs and made snow angels. When we stood up, we looked like snowmen. We laughed all the way back to the theater.

All of us in the Blackstone troupe were away from home at a time normally devoted to being with family and friends, and it had been a rough week. One of our assistants, Al Burns, quit the show to join the touring company of the musical *The Desert Song*. The men in the show had to do double cues until a new assistant could be hired. But the week ended on a bright note, because Mr. B had planned a big Christmas dinner for the entire cast, to be held at the Towne House Restaurant.

I had the best seat in the house: Blackstone Senior on one side and Blackstone Junior on the other. Every cast member received a menu with a special handwritten message from Mr. B:

> *To the Blackstone Co.*
> *This is it for Xmas directly after the matinee. My gift for your good behavior.*
> *Harry Blackstone*

I still have that menu, which included a choice of roast turkey with sage dressing or roast standing ribs of prime beef with dish gravy, along with appetizers, soup, salad, all the usual holiday side dishes, dessert, coffee, nuts and candy — all for $3.50 per person. Today we smile, but back then it was a lot of money for Blackstone to spend, and adding the five percent Massachusetts Old Age Tax, a sort of precursor to Social Security, made the bill even higher. For our group of hungry troupers, it was a lavish and much-appreciated feast.

One early afternoon in Boston, I went for a walk with no particular destination. While passing a local movie house, I noted that the next show began in ten minutes. I think I paid fifty cents admission. When the movie finished, I stayed in my seat and watched the translucent curtain close in front of the movie screen. All of a sudden, the screen rolled up, the curtain opened again, and there on the stage was the Nat King Cole Trio! In those days, it was common for big theaters to alternate movies with live stage presentations. It was an incredible thrill to sit in the audience for this unexpected and unforgettable performance. It's funny, but I can't for the life of me remember what movie I saw that day.

Philadelphia, Pennsylvania. The name of my hometown evokes a flood of memories, but right now I'll focus on just one. We were in mid-tour and had just begun a new year, 1949. My parents, ever hospitable to showfolks, invited Harry Blackstone to dinner. After we finished eating, Mr. B sat at the piano in the living room and entertained us for the rest of the evening. His favorite melody was "The Magic of Love," which he had co-written with Thomas-Ken Byron in 1939.

I hadn't known that Blackstone could play so well. Could he have made it to Carnegie Hall? I don't know. But on that occasion, it seemed to me that he commanded the keys like the wizard he was.

When I recall the people I worked with and met through my

involvement in the *Show of 1001 Wonders*, I am struck by the wonderful variety of individuals whose efforts and skills made that show such an incredible creation.

I wish I had realized, back then, what an important man Walter Gibson was. Being new to the magic scene, I did not. To me, he was Harry Blackstone's best friend, an affable, storytelling man who was fun to be around. I didn't know how famous he was. In addition to penning the radio adventures of The Shadow, Walter had known all the great magicians of the Golden Age of Magic. He'd written books for some of them. He wrote two for Blackstone.

Walter's wife was named Litzka. Her former husband had been The Great Raymond, a celebrated world-traveling conjuror — again, a fact I didn't know back then. Litzka was a magician herself, with an act that featured a rooster named China Boy. The Gibsons were guests at the Blackstone home in Michigan during the summer of 1948, when I was staying there. That summer is easy to remember, because the rooster's sleeping quarters happened to be in the closet of my room. His loud crowing at sunrise eliminated the need for an alarm clock — for me and everyone else in the house.

George A. Florida was the show's press agent and advance man. That meant he traveled ahead of the show, scheduling it into theaters, working out promotions, and visiting newsrooms to stir up interest in Blackstone. I saw Mr. Florida only a few times, on occasions when he had to consult with Mr. B about tour routes. His full name was George Alabama Florida. He reminded me of the comic-strip character Dick Tracy, because he wore a fedora hat and always had the facts about the next city on our tour. Part of his advance work was to find hotels that had reasonable prices for show people and to note nearby restaurants, then post this information on the bulletin board near the stage door of the theater. If I had known how legendary he was among press agents and journalists, and how highly regarded he was in the show world, I might have appreciated him more.

Unlike Mr. Florida, who was usually miles ahead of us, Lon Ramsdell traveled on the train with the cast. Lon was our company manager. He took care of the day-to-day concerns of the show. Among other tasks, he acted as a go-between in dealing with the local theater managers, making sure we got our share of the box-office take after the final performance had begun. Lon was a very large, bulky man who laughed uproariously at his own jokes and coughed a lot. Like many people in those days, he was a heavy smoker. Lon had one joke that he told over and over. I'll never forget it. It went like this: "Two guys are eating in a restaurant. One guy orders a tongue sandwich. The other guy says, 'I could never eat anything that came out of an animal's mouth. Give me a couple of eggs!'" And then Lon laughed and laughed.

Ward Graves was the husband of Sara Graves, the assistant I met on my first day and my "double" in some of the illusions. Ward sold Blackstone souvenir books and pocket tricks in the lobby of the theaters where we played and in the house itself at intermission. Sara, in addition to being an excellent assistant, was a perpetual knitter. That's how I remember her: knitting away as we rode the train, producing a steady stream of sweaters, scarves and mittens. She and Ward left the show after a time, and Seymour Potolsky was hired to take over the task of selling souvenir programs and small magic tricks, which was an important source of income for the show. Unlike ticket sales, money from the sales of merchandise did not have to be split with the theater.

Seymour was a nice young man from the Bronx, New York. He was slim, had dark hair, and wore black-rimmed glasses. He had a winning smile and was adventurous, always ready to discover

A change of costume in the wings. From left, Jo Habes, Mae Gallagher, and Adele in her Little Red Riding Hood outfit.

new places to see and things to do. On the train ride between engagements, Seymour and I frequently sat together, discussing our interest in museums and historical locations, and planning out the places we might like to explore when we arrived in the next city. The two of us would meet in the lobby of our hotel, have a quick breakfast in the coffee shop, and head out to catch the local bus at the corner. The cost of a roundtrip ride was usually less than 25 cents, and we could get off the bus and back on at no additional cost. Most of the time, we had no specific destination. We just rode until we found a place that looked interesting.

Whenever I took a bus ride, my favorite place to sit was in the very last seat at the back of the bus. The long back seat provided plenty of room, and the big back window offered a spacious view. Once, in the city of Atlanta, the bus that Seymour and I boarded was just starting its route, so it was empty. We went to the back seat, sat down, and continued talking. After a while, I realized that the people boarding the bus at various stops were giving us funny looks. The white folks scowled at us and then sat toward the front of the bus. The black folks stood in the aisle near the back, even though there were many open seats around us. I didn't understand it. Finally, Seymour explained to me that black people were not permitted to sit in the front of the bus or next to a white person. I looked down and noticed a line painted on the floor of the bus, dividing front from back. Segregation.

I felt guilty, like I'd done something wrong. I was in my "up North" seat, the place where I always sat when I rode the bus in Philadelphia, but this was "down South." Rosa Parks had not yet challenged the system, and civil rights legislation was more than a decade away. Today, that incident on the bus seems almost like ancient history — and I hope it is.

In the old days, the vaudeville days, every theater had its own pit band. By the time I joined the show, that was no longer true. The cost of union musicians had grown too great, and live music was required less frequently. So, each traveling show had to provide its own musical accompaniment. Our solution was to travel with an electric organ and an organist. When possible, local musicians were hired to play other instruments and give the show a fuller sound. But in some places, assembling an experienced band was impossible, so the organ was the show's only orchestra. When played by a talented organist, the electric organ could heighten the dramatic tension of a scene, accent the magical moments, and evoke any mood. It could create a soundscape that told a story. In the Elusive Moth, for instance, the organ provided the throbbing rhythm of jungle drums.

Bert Ponard was the organist for the Blackstone show when I signed on. While most of us wore casual clothes on the train, Bert was always dressed in a stylish suit and a vest. He sported a bow tie and wore a monocle attached to a fancy cord. He smoked cigarettes, blowing the smoke up and all around himself. He reminded me of an overstuffed penguin, maybe even *the* Penguin from the Batman comics.

Gladys Lyle replaced Bert after he left. She was a bright-eyed, petite woman who was a show in herself, always wearing a sparkly sequined gown when she sat at the keyboard. An artiste with immense musical talent, she bounced around as her fingers flew over the keys, and she never missed a cue. The zest with which she played added great joyousness and drama to the show.

Not only was Gladys a superb organist, she was an excellent organizer. While the show was playing in Jackson, Mississippi, some prisoners escaped from the local jail. The people of the city were warned not to travel alone on the streets, so Gladys set up a system to have us stay in groups until all the escapees were rounded up and behind bars again. In less than 24 hours, the panic alarm was off and we all thanked Gladys for watching out for our safety.

Although the world would come to know Harry Blackstone Jr. as a great magician, he was also a fine musician. That talent proved invaluable to us during our 1949 tour, when all of the sheet music for the show vanished without a trace, just a few hours before show time. Gladys could play the show music from memory, but that couldn't be expected of the local musicians who were playing in the orchestra that week. They couldn't even have a proper rehearsal without the sheet music. It was a serious predicament. Harry Junior, who had been around the show his

Among Blackstone's signature feats were intimate tricks like this one, The Floating Lightbulb.

whole life, knew the music and could name every piece and every composer. He led a search through the city's music shops to find standard sheet music — without the special arrangements that were specific to the show — for the entire orchestra. Out of all the music in the show, and there was plenty, Harry Junior managed to get sheet music for all but two pieces. That week, Gladys played solo during those two illusions.

Mr. B had many friends, all over the world, and some of them were also famous actors and entertainers. Bela Lugosi was one of Mr. B's friends. For a while, there was a rumor that the man who had played Dracula on Broadway and onscreen would be joining the Blackstone show as a guest performer for the

Halloween season and would appear in some spooky scenes. It didn't happen, although I'm told that Mr. Lugosi did tour for a while with magician Bill Neff's midnight spook show, *Madhouse of Mystery*.

Another of Blackstone's famous friends was the ventriloquist Edgar Bergen, who was an international celebrity in the days when folks gathered around the radio to listen to their favorite shows. Edgar Bergen and his sharp-tongued, wisecracking dummy Charlie McCarthy had their own weekly radio program sponsored by Chase and Sanborn Coffee, and later by Coca-Cola.

Bergen and Blackstone were both from Chicago, and whenever they were working the same cities at the same time, they arranged to meet for dinner and laughs and showbiz talk. It was great to see these two amazing performers greet each other after a show.

I'll always remember meeting Mr. Bergen for the first time. It was backstage at His Majesty's Theatre in Montreal. Every time I asked him "Where's Charlie McCarthy?" he had an answer ready. "Charlie is home helping Mortimer Snerd rehearse his stupid one-liners." It seemed a bit odd to see Edgar Bergen without Charlie McCarthy. The famous ventriloquist was hardly recognizable without his equally famous sidekick.

The art of magic might be based on secrets, but secrets are difficult to conceal among people who are living as closely together as the Blackstone cast was. One of our assistants, Loudene Power, had a secret that startled me when I accidentally discovered it. She was a truly beautiful girl, a lovely blonde who was featured in many routines in the show. I liked to watch her from the wings when she was onstage. She was shy and didn't talk with me very much. One day, I walked into the dressing room, thinking it was empty. It was not. Loudene was there — without her wig. She was bald. She had no hair of her own. We stood there and didn't say a word. I knew she was embarrassed. I hope the look in my eyes let her know that I understood and wouldn't tell the others. In fact, I've never told that story to anyone until now.

A fellow who called himself Del Ray joined the show the same week I did, the first week of October 1947. I was told that his real name was Delbert Raymond Petrosky and his home state was Ohio. One of his first duties, besides being an assistant to Blackstone, was that of "animal boy," which may evoke images of dangling from vines and swinging through the trees, but it was not as exciting as that. It meant that Del was the one who fed, watered, cleaned up after, and supervised the transportation of all the animals in the show, and there were many: a small horse (or a burro), a goat, a large gander, a brace of ducks, lots of doves, a cage full of canaries, and dozens of rabbits. This definitely was not Del's favorite chore, and he hoped another guy would soon be taking over that position.

Del preferred to focus his attention on the magic portion of the show — the props, the techniques. He worked to have everything perfect for Blackstone. Del was a fine magician in his own right, and when he was not onstage, he practiced sleight of hand with great diligence. After he left the show in late March 1949, he had a long and very successful career as one of the finest mystery performers of his day. His specialty was close-up magic and he pioneered the use of electronics in conjuring. Magicians still talk about seeing him perform, and how baffling and inspiring that was for them.

Bill Griffith was the property master for the show when I joined in Philadelphia. Bill was in his early sixties, tall, with light-brown curly hair and a smile that let you know everything was going to be okay. He was known as the Gentle Giant among the folks in the show. Bill was very conscientious when it came to making sure that all the props, large and small, were kept in good condition and were ready for use when the curtain went up.

Working a big illusion show requires a lot of energy and activity, and Bill Griffith was on his feet for many hours before, during, and after the show. Bill had trouble walking and was in constant pain. He had a severe problem with varicose veins in both legs, so he limped from place to place as best he could.

It was while we were still performing in Philadelphia that Bill finally went to see a doctor about the ever-increasing pain. The doctor told Bill to leave the show immediately and return home to Edmonton, Canada, where he could receive treatment for his legs. The problem with that plan was that Bill was in no condition to travel. Without hesitation, I spoke up. My family lived in West Philadelphia, not far from the doctor's office, and my mother was a registered nurse who could take care of Bill. To this day, I marvel at my moxie in doing that without asking my family first. My mother, father, sister and brothers welcomed Bill into our home. He stayed in the room I'd vacated when I went on tour with the show. Soon, Bill was well enough to make the trip to Canada.

Bill told his nephew Dennis Mahoney, who also lived in Edmonton, that there was an opening for an assistant on the Blackstone show. Dennis applied and was hired. As the "new guy" on the show, he was assigned to the post of animal boy. Del Ray got his wish.

Dennis loved being an onstage assistant, but did not enjoy the animal chores. He couldn't wait for the next new guy to show up and take over. As it turned out, he didn't have to wait long. Nick Ruggiero was on his way from Massachusetts to Philadelphia, where he would join the Blackstone show in January 1949.

10 · Del Ray

When the cast and crew weren't occupied with setting up, tearing down or performing the show, we spent much of our time on the train, traveling between cities. This provided Del Ray with the perfect opportunity to concentrate on his magic without interruption.

Del would retreat to the back of the train car and set up his work area. In those days, the seat backs could be moved, so folks could sit facing the front of the train or the rear. Del always pushed away the seat backs opposite to where he was sitting, so he had four seats and plenty of room. He had a small carrying case that served as a work table, a flat surface to spread out a deck of playing cards and a handful of coins, the basic tools of the close-up magician.

Del was two years my senior. He had sandy blond hair, bright blue eyes, and a unique and delightful laugh. Except for Mr. B, I never saw anyone as devoted to magic as Del was. He practiced for hours and hours. Once in a while, he would stand up and stretch, then sit right back down to his cards and coins.

One day, I asked Del if he would show me how to spread a deck of cards in a fan shape, the way magicians do before they ask someone to pick a card. Del was surprised. Then he laughed

Del Ray developed a reputation as a first-class close-up magician.

his special laugh and invited me to sit down and learn. He gave me his own deck of cards and explained that he couldn't show me how to make a card fan right away. First, I had to get a feel for handling the cards, how to hold them, how to cut them and shuffle them.

Del took this task seriously. He was a very patient teacher and encouraged me to keep going until I felt comfortable with the cards. When he was satisfied that I could handle the pack without dropping cards on the floor, he showed me how to position the deck between my left thumb and fingers, then use my right thumb to spread the cards in a circle, to the right and downward. And there it was: I was holding a lovely fan of cards in my left hand. I did this over and over again. Then I learned that if I held

Del Ray onstage with Blackstone and the Buzz Saw. Del, in costume, is peeking out from behind the giant lumber saw.

the deck in a slightly different position and used my right thumb to spread the cards upward and to the left, I could make a *reverse fan*, where all but one of the cards appeared to be blank.

Del smiled. I was on my way.

The only time Del could give me magic lessons was when we were on the train. When we were playing in a city or town, he was too busy with the show and visiting the local magic clubs with Mr. B. But before the train reached the station, Del gave me "homework" to practice and have ready for our next train ride.

Del showed me how to spring the cards between my hands, like a riverboat gambler. The goal was to shoot the cards in a steady stream from my right hand into my left, moving my hands apart and then bringing them back together again. The first fifty times I did this, the cards flew all over and had to be retrieved from under the seats of the train. Del laughed and then gave me an insider's tip. He said, "When you get to your hotel room, take a pillow and punch a big dent in it. Put the pillow in the middle of the bed, then practice springing the cards into the dent. You'll get the feel for how to shoot the cards from the bottom of the deck, directly into a target." This was a great idea, because if — more like *when* — the cards went astray, I wouldn't have to pick them up off the floor.

With a dented pillow and lots of practice, I learned to spring the cards pretty well. I even gained enough confidence to try spreading the deck in a neat ribbon up the middle of my left arm, from wrist to elbow. I never got that to work, though. The cards always fell off.

A move I called "hide the card" was next. I learned later that magicians call it the back palm. This involves holding a card at the fingertips and then shifting the card to a position where it's hidden behind the hand. I practiced this in front of a mirror in my hotel room. Even though I was a thin girl, I didn't have bony fingers. There were no spaces between my fingers when I held them together, which made it easier for me to hide a card behind them. Eventually, I could do this quite well, but I could never back palm more than one card. Del could back palm many cards and then make them appear, one at a time. Like everything else he did, he made it look effortless.

I asked Del if he could teach me how to roll a coin over the knuckles of my hand, a mesmerizing little flourish I had seen him do. He handed me a fifty-cent piece and showed me the basic moves. Before long, I was running that coin across my knuckles, catching it, then pushing it past my palm and up to the starting position for another run, all with one hand.

Del's "go for it" attitude, his encouragement to keep working and not give up, made almost anything seem possible, given enough time and effort. That's the real lesson I learned from my teacher, Del Ray. No wonder he loved magic so much.

11 · Atlanta, 1949

Annie Get Your Gun might not be the first thing that comes to mind when you think of Atlanta, Georgia. But it does for me, because we saw that wonderful stage musical while we were there. The road-show cast of *Annie Get Your Gun* happened to be staying at the same hotel we were — the Georgian Terrace. We all got acquainted and they arranged for us to see the show. We couldn't go in the evening, because we had a show of our own to do, so we went to a matinee during the off hours before our evening performance. I can still hear those great Irving Berlin tunes playing in my mind, especially the high-spirited *There's No Business Like Show Business*. Hear that song once and you'll never forget it. I liked it so much, I'd used it for the closing number in my dance act.

We returned the favor by inviting the cast of *Annie Get Your Gun* to our show. As it turned out, though, those folks didn't get a chance to see all the magical marvels we'd promised them.

We thought Blackstone was just late getting to the theater. The show was ready to go, everything was set: silks, props, animals in place, costumed assistants onstage. To stall for time, Gladys Lyle played every show tune she could remember. We could hear the audience becoming restless. Still, we thought Mr. B would arrive at the last minute, throw on his costume, and dash out onto the stage.

Word came that Blackstone was not just late; he'd been admitted to Crawford Long Hospital. Pete dropped everything and rushed to be with his brother. We all knew that a severe asthma attack could be fatal.

The people in the audience were not told how serious the situation was. They were simply informed that the great magician was ill and could not perform the show. Their surprise and disappointment at hearing this news was evidenced by a long, collective intake of breath. Ironically, it was the kind of sound that Harry Blackstone could not make.

We didn't need to be told that the 1949 tour was finished. We only hoped that Mr. B would be okay.

12 · BLACKSTONE ISLAND

For the second season in a row, the tour ended abruptly. The rest of our bookings were canceled. On March 29, we received our final pay — in cash, as usual — along with money for transportation home.

Del Ray and I said goodbye. Before we left, he gave me his home address in Hubbard, Ohio. I never wrote to him. I wish I had. I have no explanation except to say that, in true show-business fashion, I dismissed the past; and in true young-person fashion, I gave no thought to the future except as it concerned my own affairs. More than fifty years would pass before I spoke with Del again, in June 2003. And, sadly, I would never have another opportunity. Del passed away just five months after our long phone conversation.

At the train station in Atlanta, Pete Bouton made sure all the gear was loaded in the baggage cars. Some of the cast would ride that train back to Michigan and Blackstone Island.

Sally Banks was the person who kept the Blackstone homestead in ship-shape while Mr. B was on the road. She had been born Della Cowell, but everyone in showbiz called her Sally Banks. She'd been a part-time nanny for Harry Junior when he was a child, and she was the year-round housekeeper and caretaker at

Blackstone Island. The vagabonds from the 1949 tour would be welcome there.

I didn't go to Michigan. Instead, I returned to Philadelphia to take up my song-and-dance act again. I was lucky to be able to fall back on nightclub gigs. To tell the truth, with Mr. B being so hard-hit in Atlanta, I had my doubts that the Blackstone show would ever travel again. But in July, I received a letter from Fred Phillips, indicating that the show was going back on tour:

July 20, 1949

Dear Adele:
Please come to Colon at once as all the kids will be here, and Adele call Irene, so you two can come together.
I think Sturgis is your best bet.
Please will meet you so wire what time your train gets in.

Freddie

"Irene" was Irene Holt. We had worked together as assistants and sometimes we'd been roommates. We didn't end up traveling to Michigan together as Fred suggested, because she'd made other arrangements — arrangements that probably involved Harold Swartzenburg, the electrician on the show, whom she would eventually marry. Today, I wonder how their marriage worked out. Harold was a heavy drinker and he had a quick temper. One night, after the show, he had a few drinks too many and got into a fight in a restaurant. It wasn't the first time Harold had been drunk and out of control in public. The Boss expected us to act as representatives of the Blackstone company, whether we were onstage or off. He wouldn't tolerate behavior that could give the show a bad reputation. So he fired Harold on the spot. Unfortunately, this caused Mr. B and his brother to

Looking down at Blackstone's home on the "island." Sturgeon Lake lies in the distance.

be at odds. Pete and Millie Bouton were Harold's friends; they thought Mr. B had overreacted. Tension ruled the day. Onstage, everything looked fine. But backstage, the Blackstone show was filled with whispers and avoided glances. People took sides. A rumor circulated that Pete and Millie were leaving the show. At last, after some serious talks, the brothers were able to work out their differences. Things went back to normal. Pete and Millie stayed with the show.

Back in the summer of 1949, I couldn't have guessed that all that drama lay ahead. All I knew was that I was on my way to Blackstone Island to begin rehearsals for the new tour.

Blackstone Island was the name given to the 208 acres of Mr. B's property, which was just outside the main village and fronted by Sturgeon Lake. Appropriately enough for a magical place, things were not quite as they seemed: Sturgeon Lake was not really a lake, and Blackstone Island was not really an island. The lake, as Fred had explained to me on my first journey to the Blackstone homestead, was simply a very wide bend in the St. Joseph River. And although Blackstone Island was surrounded by water — the lake-like expanse in front and narrow creeks on the remaining sides — it was an island in name only.

Mr. B was known for his expertise in turning the ordinary into the grandiose — I had heard Millie Bouton refer to him as "that bullshitter"— but he was also a very generous man. At Blackstone Island, bed and board were free. On a bluff overlooking the lake were fishermen's shacks that Pete and Mr. B had converted into mini-dormitories for the cast. The dorms provided a place to sleep — simple beds, no cooking facilities. At mealtimes, everyone gathered at the big kitchen table in Blackstone's home, like a family. Whatever the Boss had, everyone had. The menus were simple but delicious: scrambled eggs, toast and coffee for breakfast; soups, sandwiches and salads for lunch; steaks, chops, roasts, fresh fish and casseroles for dinner.

I returned to Blackstone Island in August 1949. I dropped off my suitcase in the girls' dorm. Mae Gallagher was already there. When I asked her where her husband Frank was staying, she gave me a doleful look and said, "He's in the boys' dorm." The division between the sexes had been set up in the days when most of the assistants were single. But I'm sure Mae and Frank found a way to work it out.

I headed to the red barn, where I was surprised to see Mr. B busily working on a project with Pete and a male assistant. I knew that the Boss had recovered from his asthma attack in Atlanta, but I'd expected to see him resting and recouping his strength in anticipation of the tour. Instead, he was back at work. And to be honest, he looked to be in the best of health. I later learned that, after his hospital stay in Georgia, he had gone to an asthma clinic in Mississippi, where the latest medical

A picture postcard view of Blackstone's home and garden, taken from the lake.

treatments were available. They had discovered a way to control the malady.

In ones and twos, the Blackstone cast assembled at the Island. Some folks were perennials. Some were brand new. In the daytime, we worked to prepare and rehearse every illusion for our tour. In the evenings, we were never too worn out to find our way to an outlying roadhouse for a late snack and some country dancing.

August in Michigan can bring heavy thunderstorms, and we certainly had our share. Suddenly, a bright blue sky would darken until it seemed like night. Lightning flashed, thunder crashed, and then came the downpour. After the storms, we could smell the sweet aroma of mint drifting in from the fields. Many acres of Blackstone's land were set aside for cultivating mint. The Wrigley Company of Chicago used those tiny leaves to flavor their chewing gum.

When I wasn't painting props or rehearsing my cues, I spent a good part of my time helping Sally Banks prepare meals and do other chores. I got to know her quite well. Sally couldn't have been more than five feet in height. She joined the Blackstone show in 1927 and performed as a box jumper for thirteen seasons. She'd been married to Ted Banks, who was Blackstone's stage manager for many years. Ted's real name was Edward Coppin. He died on September 3, 1942, the day after he and Blackstone helped to save hundreds of people — most of them children — from the fumes of a chemical fire in a building next to the Lincoln Theatre in Decatur, Illinois. The stress of that ordeal was probably what killed Ted Banks.

In 1940, Sally was in a terrible car accident. She recovered, but she could no longer squeeze into illusion cabinets. So she dived into her new roles as housekeeper, caretaker, nanny, and chief cook — and she performed every one of them with gusto. The range of her culinary knowhow was enormous. And she had the temperament of a seasoned trouper: nothing seemed to faze her.

In September 1949, we packed up the show and left Blackstone Island for Milwaukee, Wisconsin. September 9 and 10 were devoted to dress rehearsals at the Davidson Theatre, followed by opening night and the start of a seven-day run. The Elusive Moth was a big hit with the audiences. And this was just the first stop on an ambitious tour of 46 cities, 10 shows a week, scheduled from September 11, 1949 to April 1, 1950.

An unspoken question hovered in the air: *Will we complete this tour?*

13 · 1001 Wonders

A reviewer once wrote that "Seeing the Blackstone Magic Show is like riding a tidal wave of wonder, laughter, and delight." I knew that was true, even though I never saw the show from the audience. Decades after I left the stage to pursue other paths, I would have my first opportunity to see some of the show, including a teenage version of myself, through the magic of film.

Back when I was in the show, I was too busy onstage and backstage — listening for cues, changing costumes, hiding in secret compartments, jumping out of boxes, crawling behind various concealments, carrying props from place to place — to think about what the performance looked like from the point of view of the house. But I could hear the gasps of astonishment, the laughs, the cheers and applause. And I could see Blackstone's look of satisfaction when everything was going well.

Our 1949–1950 tour began with a bang. We played to sell-out crowds everywhere we went: Milwaukee, Kansas City, Des Moines, St. Joseph, Salina, Wichita, Hutchinson, Topeka. In every city, I twirled and leaped and danced as the Elusive Moth, then I vanished in a puff of smoke.

A studio photo showing elements of the Enchanted Garden sequence. Early 1940s.

The opening scene of *Blackstone's Show of 1001 Wonders* was one of my favorites. It was called the Enchanted Garden, and I liked it for its beauty as well as its magic.

All twelve assistants took part in the opening number. Dressed in Colonial costumes, the assistants struck a pose while Blackstone entered in his white tie and tails and satin-lined cape, immediately tossing his gloves into the air, where they became fluttering white doves. He made roses bloom from a bouquet of greenery he held in his hands, then he magically produced an endless array of flowers to fill his garden. One by one, the bouquets were tossed toward the stage floor, where they stuck, upright, surrounding us with the bright colors of springtime.

Blackstone presented a bouquet to each of the girl assistants.

I left the stage with my flowers and, in mere moments, returned in a different costume, carrying the empty circular frame of a tambourine. I held the frame steady while Blackstone quickly fastened tissue paper over both sides. He punched a hole in the tissue, reached in, and pulled out a handful of small, colorful silk handkerchiefs, followed by a gigantic silk cloth. He held up the cloth for a moment, ostensibly so the audience could appreciate the colorful design, but really to hide me from view. When the cloth was whisked away, I was a rose bush.

Next, Blackstone gestured for a giant cone to be shown empty and then lowered over a girl wearing a two-piece costume. The magician gestured again. Up went the cone, revealing that the girl had turned into a flowering tree.

To complete the Enchanted Garden tableau, a tiered fountain appeared, spraying real water.

But that was just the beginning.

The Blackstone show was known for having top-notch production values. The costumes were as much a part of the spectacle as the magic. Every time a female assistant was offstage, she had a costume change. When the audience saw her a few minutes later, she was wearing a completely different outfit — even if all she did was a walk-on, carrying a prop to Mr. B and then dashing off into the wings.

After big production numbers like the Enchanted Garden or the Elusive Moth, Blackstone performed smaller routines "in one," between the main curtain and the footlights. This allowed time for the stage to be cleared and for props to be placed. My Lady's Garter was one of those transitional numbers, a quick magic routine that Blackstone and I worked together. I walked out to center stage, carrying a tray on which rested a box. The box was decorated with red velvet; it looked as if it might contain a magical artifact or a romantic gift — or both! Blackstone picked up the box, opened it, and showed a glittering garter inside. He

Blackstone smiles as the garter appears on the leg of Mary Harris.

closed the lid with an emphatic *snap* and then, a second later, opened it again. The garter was gone. Proudly, he pointed to my left leg. There, sparkling and shining, was the garter. I gave a look of surprise, smiled, tossed my head, and exited stage right. Applause.

For the Garter routine, I wore either a pale-blue or deep-red velvet costume, depending on which one was back from the cleaners. The dress was short, like a dancer's costume. After all, my legs had to be seen.

Once, in my first season with the show, I failed to properly activate the gimmick that caused the garter to reappear, so instead of showing up on my leg, it fell to the stage. I picked it up, waved it above my head, smiled, and walked into the wings.

When I turned around and looked back toward the stage, the Boss was still staring at me, shaking his mop of white hair and smiling at what I'd just done. The trick never went wrong again.

When I joined the show in 1947, the Hindu Rope Mystery was on the program. I remember watching it as I stood in the wings. A basket with a coiled rope inside was center stage. Blackstone beckoned, and a boy wearing a white Indian turban ran out from backstage and stood near the basket. The eerie sound of a flute was heard. The music grew louder and louder while the magician waved his hand and caused the rope to rise out of the basket. With the rope standing straight up in the air, the boy was commanded to climb up. As he neared the top, there was a puff of smoke, and the boy was gone. Of course, watching from the wings, I could see plenty of things the audience couldn't. Still, it was an impressive mood piece, sort of a precursor to the Elusive Moth.

The Crystal Casket illusion was a dazzler. When the curtain opened, assistants Nick Ruggiero and Del Ray, wearing white gloves, pushed a flat platform on wheels to center stage. Two more assistants, Frank Gallagher and Tom Reid, also wearing white gloves, rolled out a rack that held panes of plate glass. At Blackstone's direction, the first piece of glass was gently lifted and placed flat on the platform. Then, two smaller pieces were positioned upright at both ends of the first pane. Two large pieces were added on the remaining sides, and when the final piece was placed on top, it was a large glass box — a Crystal Casket.

A beautiful silk cloth was draped over the box. The four men spun the platform around once. With a grand gesture, Blackstone swept the cloth away. Inside the Crystal Casket was Betty Stolle, wearing a sparkling silver costume. Blackstone lifted the glass lid, took her hand, and guided her out for a bow. I was standing in the wings, waiting for my next walk-on, and I marveled at what a startling illusion this was. Sometimes, I couldn't help but wish that I were the girl in the shining silver sequins.

A sequin-covered girl appears in the Crystal Casket. Early 1940s.

And now, a riddle: *How can a person have been featured in a stage illusion and not have any idea what it looked like?*

This riddle involves me and the Costume Trunk illusion, so I can tell you the answer: *Because I was hidden until the very end and couldn't see what was going on.*

The Costume Trunk illusion began with a platform being rolled onstage by Nick Ruggiero and Frank Gallagher. Del Ray and Fred Phillips carried in a number of rectangular wooden drawers that were filled with various costumes. The drawers were stacked up, one on top of the other, on the platform. A four-sided enclosure was dropped over the stack of drawers, and a top was added, so it looked like a costume trunk.

At stage left was a small table that supported a vase with flowers in it. Next to the table was a clothes rack, attached to which were five large dolls dressed as recognizable characters: a circus clown, Raggedy Ann, a toy soldier, Little Red Riding Hood, and Alice in Wonderland.

With a nearby assistant holding a rifle, Blackstone asked for a volunteer from the audience to come up to the stage "for some target practice." There was always someone eager to oblige. Everyone onstage stood back while the volunteer took aim at a doll of his choosing. The first "shot" always hit the vase of flowers, causing it to crash to the stage. While the audience laughed at this apparent mistake, Blackstone feigned dismay and took back the rifle. With tongue firmly in cheek, the magician ordered the man to stand aside and called for another volunteer. This time it worked: the volunteer fired a shot, and one of the dolls dropped off the rack. It was the doll dressed as Little Red Riding Hood.

Immediately, Blackstone strode to the trunk, threw back the lid, and up I popped, dressed as — who else? — Little Red Riding Hood. Blackstone took my hand and helped me out of the trunk, twirled me around to show off my costume, bowed graciously, and sent me dancing offstage.

Before every performance of the Costume Trunk, Nick and I discussed what I planned to wear. Would I be Alice in Wonderland or Little Red Riding Hood? He was the one who set up the falling doll, so he had to know ahead of time.

When I appeared in an illusion called The Drum That Can't Be Beat, I was dressed in a colorful peasant costume. Mae Gallagher was the "regular" in that illusion, and when she and her husband Frank left the show, Irene Holt took over. It was a rule that every illusion must have a girl on standby, in case the regular girl had to miss a performance. I was the standby for this illusion and worked it a number of times.

To the rousing melody of "Strike Up the Band," two male assistants rolled out a stand on which sat the shell of a big bass drum. The audience could see that the drum shell was empty. Two large sheets of paper were displayed, then Blackstone

The final production from The Drum That Can't Be Beat was a member of the Blackstone company.

attached these to both ends of the drum, securing them in place with hoops. Chains were lowered from above and attached to the sides of the drum. The chains were used to lift the drum up and off the stand. With the drum suspended over the stage, the stand was rolled away.

Blackstone used his fingers to poke a hole in the paper. Then another. And another. When the audience realized that the holes formed a large smiley face on the front of the drum, it got a big laugh. Blackstone reached into the perforations and drew out two strings of multicolored flags. Assistants grabbed the ends and ran down the stage steps and up the aisles, with the long strings of flags streaming out behind them. At that point, the audience was clapping in time with the music.

The flags were gathered up and brought back onstage just as Trixie the Horse appeared suddenly at stage right. At the same time, Gandy the Gander appeared at stage left, squawking and flapping his wings. The pandemonium reached a peak when Blackstone tore open the paper drumhead and pulled out one of the show's Gorgeous Girls.

All that color and action and sound — the flags, the animals, the music, the girl — was combined with baffling magic and whipped up into a perfect piece of showmanship, guaranteed to bring audiences to their feet.

The Dream of Princess Karnac was a wonderful mystery that never failed to amaze the crowd. Among magicians in America, this illusion was known as the Kellar Levitation. Ironically, Kellar was the man who stole the secret of the illusion from its inventor, a British magician named Maskelyne.

The Princess Karnac levitation took so much time to set up, we could do it only in towns where we played longer than one day. It was a marvel of magical ingenuity. The stage could be in full light, the Princess needed no covering whatsoever, and still the laws of gravity seemed to be defied.

Betty Stolle played the Princess. She arrived onstage like royalty, in a sedan chair carried by two assistants. Blackstone guided her out and then hypnotized her until she fell into a deep trance. She was placed gently on a couch. As the master magician wove a tale of strange goings-on in the Himalayas, Princess Karnac began to float up into the air. The couch was removed. Blackstone gestured for the Princess to stop rising. A large hoop was brought onstage, and Blackstone did a beautiful hoop-sweep over and around her to show that there were no wires above or below. Then she rose again, higher and higher, until Blackstone commanded her to float down toward the stage. The couch was rolled beneath her, she made a soft landing, and she was awakened to take a bow. I can still hear Blackstone telling

Bunny Luckner played the role of Princess Karnac in Blackstone's levitation illusion of the same name.

the audience that the Dream of Princess Karnac was "something you will remember to the longest day you live." And so it was.

Recently, through a surprising string of events, I had the opportunity to speak with Bunny Luckner, who was Princess Karnac in the Blackstone show from 1935–1939. Bunny told me that the two pieces of music for the levitation, "Meditation" and "Romance," were quite soothing and relaxing, and she really felt like she was floating.

Another all-time great illusion was The Sepoy Mutiny, sometimes known as The Mystery of Delhi. The setting was an open marketplace, crowded with people in native dress. My costume was shining gold. I led Trixie the Horse (or Sally the Burro) across the stage to add activity to the background of the scene. As I exited, a stage fight broke out. Blackstone was seized and lashed to the mouth of a cannon. The fuse was lit. The cannon roared. When the cloud of smoke cleared, the magician was nowhere to be seen. Had he perished in the blast? The man who fired the cannon stepped forward and threw off his robe. It was Blackstone himself!

In happy contrast to the sound and fury of the previous scene, Blackstone's presentation of The Boy and Rabbit was a playful routine that allowed him to interact with a child from the audience. Despite the title, Blackstone often chose a girl for this one. As the curtains closed behind him, the magician walked forward with something cradled in his hands. It was a tiny bunny rabbit. He called out to the audience, "I'm going to give this little rabbit to the first boy or girl who says 'I.'" Of course, all of the children screamed "I," which made the theater fill with laughter. After asking "Who said it first?" and "Who said it last?" accompanied by more screams and laughter, Blackstone selected a young girl, maybe eight or nine years old, to join him onstage. As she was leaving her row of seats, Blackstone got permission from the parents for her to have the rabbit.

Once she was on the stage, that child never took her eyes off the rabbit. Nothing else in the world was important. She wanted the bunny. As soon as she reached for it, Blackstone suggested that they should wrap up the bunny so she could hold it on her lap for the rest of the show. He called for an assistant to bring out a few sheets of newspaper. The girl helped Blackstone wrap up the rabbit. Then, clutching the package close to her heart, she started to leave the stage.

"Stop!" shouted Blackstone with comical disdain. "Do you know what you have done?" The girl froze in surprise. Blackstone

A delighted youngster receives a Blackstone bunny.

told her that she had squeezed the rabbit; she was "a rabbit squeezer." The child denied the accusation, so Blackstone told her to unwrap the rabbit. Inside the newspaper was a box of chocolates. The bunny was gone.

Blackstone told the girl that she could keep the chocolates, then he called for the "story steps" to be brought in. The set of three steps was slipped through the opening at the center of the main curtain. Blackstone took the girl's hand and guided her to the top step, where they both sat down. The magician began to tell a fairy tale. But the girl didn't want chocolates or a fairy tale. She wanted a rabbit. Blackstone said, "I'll make a paper rabbit for you." He called for more newspaper, which he rolled into a ball. "This is a paper mâché rabbit, which means it is mashed." So saying, he smashed the paper ball. The little girl looked horrified.

But wait — something seemed to be materializing from the

Children crowd Blackstone, placing hands on the birdcage before it vanishes for a second time.

paper. First, a bunny's tail. Then, a pair of ears. And finally, a real live rabbit. Blackstone put the rabbit on top of the box of chocolates, placed the girl's hand on top of the rabbit so it wouldn't fall off, and sent the happiest kid in the world back to her seat.

The Vanishing Birdcage was another crowd-pleaser. Blackstone walked out with a small cage held in his hands. A yellow bird was inside. "I'll make this cage vanish from the tips of my fingers," said the magician, "and you'll not see where it goes." He motioned as if to fling the cage into the air. Instead, the cage and the bird vanished in an instant.

"I'll get another cage, another canary, and do it again," Blackstone promised. He stepped behind the curtain for a moment, then walked out with a new cage. This time, Mr. B invited children from the audience to place their hands on the cage and prevent it from vanishing. A stampede of kids came up onstage. Blackstone instructed some of the children to put their hands on top of the cage, some on the bottom of the cage, and some on the sides. The remaining children were told to put their hands on top of the other kids' hands.

With the cage surrounded by a cluster of hands, there seemed to be no way for it vanish. But vanish it did. Suddenly, the cage and the bird weren't there. The youngsters looked all around Blackstone and all over the stage. The birdcage couldn't be found. To a big round of applause, the mystified kids were sent back to sit with the mystified grownups.

Magicians might wonder why I haven't mentioned two of Blackstone's best-known routines: the Floating Light Bulb and the Dancing Handkerchief. The answer is that I never had a chance to see Blackstone perform those two classics of magic, because I appeared in the scenes right before and after them. Mr. B kept the basic show order the same from year to year, so I was always busy changing costumes and hiding in cabinets while the light bulb floated and the handkerchief danced.

Oklahoma City, Tulsa, Springfield, St. Louis, Pittsburgh, Columbus, Cleveland. Blackstone was in top form and showed no sign of slowing down. Toledo, Rochester, Buffalo, Wilmington, and a merry Christmas in Philadelphia with my family. Then onward to Baltimore, where Mr. B and a bunch of us from the cast attended the christening of a baby boy, the son of Raymond Corbin, otherwise known as the magician Ray-Mond. On December 31, at the local assembly of the Society of American Magicians, the boy was christened David Blackstone Corbin.

The old year became a new year, 1950, and the Blackstone show was still going strong. Richmond, Charleston, Indianapolis, Louisville, Lexington. It was beginning to look like our luck would hold out and we'd finish the tour.

14 · A Chinese Fantasy

The first act of the Blackstone show featured a scene called A Chinese Fantasy. It deserves a chapter of its own, because it was actually four illusions packed into one fast-moving, eye-catching series of surprises.

Imagine that you're sitting in a plush seat in a lovely theater. Maybe it's the Lyceum in Minneapolis, or the Davidson in Milwaukee, or the Lyric in Allentown. Blackstone has you under his spell. A garden of flowers magically appears on the stage. A borrowed pocket handkerchief springs to life and dances around like a mischievous spirit. And now…

The curtains open to show an old-fashioned Chinese setting. Up-tempo music — including renditions of "In Old Chinatown," "China Boy," and "Limehouse Blues" — sets a brisk pace, putting an extra spring in Blackstone's step as he strides forward, smiling at the audience. Nick Ruggiero, dressed in Chinese costume, enters from stage right. He carries a long bamboo pole over his right shoulder as he passes by Blackstone. A large birdcage hangs from each end of the pole — one in front, one behind. White doves flutter in the front cage. Suddenly, a white-plumed fan appears in Blackstone's hand. With a graceful gesture, the magician sweeps the fan past the front cage, and the birds disappear. He then fans the second cage, and the doves reappear.

Blackstone turns to see two male assistants, also dressed in Chinese costume, rolling out a wide wooden cabinet on spindly legs. The cabinet is whirled around and then placed center stage. An assistant lifts the top of the cabinet, and Blackstone opens the front. A decorative Chinese scene has been painted on the interior of the cabinet, but nothing else is inside. The cabinet is closed again.

Two more assistants carry a gigantic Chinese lantern onto the stage. The lantern is collapsed flat and placed on top of the cabinet. A trapeze is lowered and its chains are hooked to the sides of the lantern. Blackstone sweeps his hand upward; the lantern unfurls, covering the trapeze bar, as it is hoisted high above the stage.

A girl enters from stage right. She is dressed in a two-piece outfit: a blue top with gold brocade, long sleeves, and a high-necked collar in the Chinese style, and blue pants with gold Chinese characters at the cuffs. Black slippers are on her feet, and a little pillbox hat completes the look. The girl carries a striped cloth bag, which she hands to Blackstone. The top of the cabinet is opened, the bag is placed inside, and two assistants lift the girl into the cabinet. The bag is pulled up around the girl. Blackstone uses a length of cord to tie the top of the bag. He closes the cabinet, and it is spun around once more. When Blackstone opens the cabinet, there's nothing inside but an empty cloth bag with the rope still knotted around it. The girl is gone.

As the assistants move the cabinet offstage left, a lovely tall girl — Merle Norton — enters stage right. She is dressed in an elaborate Chinese costume that features an immense headpiece decorated with red and gold jewels, colorful plumes, and pheasant feathers. She holds a Chinese gong, ready to strike it on Blackstone's cue.

A scene from the Chinese Fantasy. The girl in the "Up-and-Down" is about to disappear.

Wham! The sound of the gong reverberates throughout the theater. The gigantic lantern drops to the stage floor. Blackstone gestures upward. There, smiling radiantly on the trapeze bar, sits the girl who vanished from the striped cloth bag.

The trapeze lowers so Blackstone can take the girl's hand and give her a twirl and a running leap onto a new illusion that has been moved into place. Folks in the show refer to this illusion as "the Up-and-Down." The base consists of a flat three-foot-square platform on legs, so the audience can see underneath it. Four metal poles, each twelve feet high, stand at the corners of the platform. A heavy wooden canopy, the same size as the platform, is positioned at the top of the four poles. The girl smiles and stands on the platform, hands on her hips. A curtain is lowered from the canopy, completely surrounding the girl.

Wham! The gong is struck again, and suddenly the canopy crashes down onto the platform below. The girl who was standing there a moment ago has magically disappeared. It's one of the most impossible-looking illusions in the show.

The platform is wheeled off into the wings while a huge, brightly colored "flower pot" is brought to the center of the stage. The four sides of the flower pot open outward and downward, so it can be shown empty. The audience sees nothing inside, so the four sections of the flower pot are swung back up into their original positions. The assistants give the illusion a quick spin. At Blackstone's command, the sides of the flower pot are opened, and the missing girl reappears once more. She jumps out and takes a bow with the master magician who made the Fantasy a reality.

The Chinese Fantasy sequence is a perfect example of the Blackstone style. While many magicians would have presented those illusions separately, Blackstone combined them into a whirlwind of magic and surprise. His show was seamless. There was something happening at every moment. And that required split-second timing on everyone's part.

Moments before A Chinese Fantasy begins, I climb into the cabinet — the one with the spindly legs. I can hear the music, so I know when the birds have reappeared in the second birdcage and it's time for the cabinet to be wheeled onstage. My castmates push the cabinet out, spin it around, and position it exactly where it should be. No surprises.

One assistant lifts the lid while another assistant secretly drops the back of the cabinet, forming a little shelf. The rear wall of the cabinet, with the decorative scene painted on it, is actually

Blackstone poses with the cabinet on the "spindly legs." Janie Hays is inside. Studio photo ca. 1946.

a canvas curtain. I lift the curtain and roll under it. There's just enough room on the shelf for me to scrunch down and remain hidden behind the cabinet. With one of my hands, I hold the curtain taut while Blackstone opens the drop-down front of the cabinet, showing it empty. When the doors are closed, I roll back inside. An assistant returns the shelf to the upright position as I get ready for my next move.

The decorative painting on the inside of the cabinet extends right up onto the lid. The painting disguises a hidden door in the top of the cabinet. The giant lantern is collapsed flat and placed on the lid while the trapeze is lowered. Blackstone says the word "right" when the trapeze is hooked to the lantern. That's my cue to scramble through the hidden door, up and out of the cabinet, and onto the trapeze. I only have seconds to accomplish this, because the trapeze is already in motion when I climb onto it.

Hidden inside the lantern, I'm lifted to a position high above the stage. I pull my legs up as far as possible, so the audience can't see my feet. From my perch, I can see Sara Graves walk right under the lantern, holding the striped cloth bag in her hands. She's wearing a costume that is identical to mine. This is one of the illusions in which Sara and I are doubles — secret twins. So far, I've been onstage for several minutes, inside two different pieces of equipment, and no one in the audience knows I'm there. In a moment, Sara will be placed into the cabinet that I just vacated, then she'll vanish away.

Meanwhile, I prepare for my appearance by grasping two little rubber bulbs that are attached to the chains of the trapeze. When Merle Norton hits the gong, I squeeze the bulbs, releasing the lantern so it falls to the stage. *And here I am*, sitting on the trapeze bar, swinging my legs and smiling at the audience. I look exactly like Sara Graves. The audience applauds as the trapeze is lowered to the stage.

Keeping up with the rhythm of the music, Blackstone twirls me around and we do a short run so he can "airlift" me onto the platform of the Up-and-Down. I stand on the platform with my feet apart and my fists on my hips, like Yul Brynner in *The King and I*. A curtain drops around the illusion. I use my foot to press down on the middle section of the floor, which opens a cavity big enough for me to squeeze into so I'll be out of harm's way. The area where I hide is about eight inches deep. I weigh less than 100 pounds and my body is very flexible, so I can flatten myself into the tiny space.

The gong is struck again. The canopy crashes down above me. The audience gasps. And then I feel the platform being pushed offstage.

As I climb out of my hiding place in the Up-and-Down, Sara Graves is about to make her reappearance from the flower pot. She's the lucky girl who will hold Blackstone's hand and take the bow for both of us. There's not even time for me to watch the end of the routine. I have a costume change to make.

In the hundreds of shows we did, only once was there a problem during the Chinese Fantasy number. I had been with the show about two weeks. While I was climbing out of the hidden door in the lid of the cabinet, up and onto the trapeze that was already being hoisted into the air, my costume got stuck on the door. I said "wait," loud enough for my castmates to hear. Blackstone misheard this as "right," the word that was the signal for "everything is okay." But everything wasn't okay. I was stuck. One of the male assistants did some quick thinking and brought the lantern down low enough for the other assistant to get me loose. This all took about ten seconds. But for the Boss, who was a perfectionist, that was ten seconds too long. I heard him say a few choice words under his breath. When the gong sounded and I appeared on the trapeze, swinging my legs and smiling, Blackstone was smiling too. He gave my hand an extra squeeze before he twirled me over to the next illusion.

Other than the star himself, I believe I am the only cast member who spoke a line during the Blackstone show. And that was only when the limitations of the theater would not allow us to hang the trapeze for the big lantern. On those rare occasions, instead of appearing on the trapeze, I had to race out the stage door, dash around to the front of the theater and through the lobby, and slip into the back of the auditorium to make my surprise appearance. Here's how it went:

Sara Graves vanished from the cloth bag inside the cabinet.
Blackstone bellowed, "Where is she?"
I answered in a loud voice "Here I am, Mr. Blackstone!" as I

ran down the aisle and up to the stage, so I could take my position on the platform of the Up-and-Down.

One time, as I rushed through the theater lobby on my way to deliver my only line, an overzealous usher stopped me, told me that there was a performance in progress, and refused to let me into the theater without a ticket. The only way I could prove to him that I was needed onstage in a minute was to take off my cape and show him my costume. He tried to apologize, but there was no time. I tossed the cape to him, and ran down the aisle while saying my line. The usher met me after the show to return my cape.

15 · Exit, Stage Left

On April 1, 1950, we played our closing engagement in Bay City, Michigan. No trips to the hospital. No sudden cancellations. The tour finished as planned.

We'd been on the road since September 9, 1949. We'd played 22 states and 46 cities, with close to 250 performances. And even though we were pleased by what we'd accomplished, no one was sorry to see the season come to an end. We were tired. We wanted to go home.

There were no sentimental goodbyes. I suppose we figured we would be back together again for the next season, so why make a big thing out of the usual summer break?

We should have noted the date. April Fool's Day. Fate had a couple of tricks up its sleeve.

I returned to Philadelphia with two objectives in mind: first, to get reacquainted with my family; and second, to reactivate my song-and-dance act.

Catching up on missed time with my brothers and my sister, who all seemed to have grown up so quickly while I was away, was a fairly simple task. But my second goal was another matter. Reviving my dance career was difficult — *very* difficult — because

I'd been out of circulation for so long. In ordinary life, eight months is a short time, but it's an eternity to theatrical booking agents. So I really knuckled down and pushed hard to reestablish the act. I put together new dance routines, got flashier costumes, and put pressure on agents to let them know that I was back and ready to work.

Maybe I shouldn't have tried so hard. I succeeded, but too well.

I got a string of choice engagements at inns and resorts in the Pennsylvania coal country — a full week in each location. At one of the inns, the floor was so bad that I shouldn't have danced on it. I tried to, though. I leaped. I twirled. I fell. It wasn't just a simple spill. I crashed down like a rock. My leg was twisted so severely, they had to carry me off and cut the shoe ribbons away from my swollen ankle.

There went the rest of my bookings. I couldn't even walk without pain, let alone dance.

I was still recuperating when the letter came. It was from Harry Blackstone, written in his hand, and sent from a New York City hotel. I'd been dreading this moment, and here it was, the question I didn't want to face: *The show is opening on October 2. Will you be available?*

It tied me in knots to think of someone else dancing the role of the Elusive Moth. But I had to say no.

And here's where Fate, that old April Fooler, does some more sleight of hand. I don't believe Blackstone ever made that tour. There's no evidence that the show opened in October or at any other time that season.

What happened? Was he unable to gather a suitable cast? US military forces had conscripted many young men for the Korean War. Nick Ruggiero was no longer a magician's assistant, he was a soldier.

Or did Blackstone just change his mind?

I don't know. What I *do* know, having learned it only recently,

Singing and dancing again, this time at a Christmas show in Philadelphia.

is that in November 1950, in Chicago, Blackstone married his third wife, Elizabeth Ross. Shortly thereafter, he put the show in storage, sold his property in Michigan, and moved to New York City.

My castmates and I didn't realize that we were making history. That show in Bay City on April Fool's Day was the last of the big Blackstone magic shows — the very last. Never again would the *Show of 1001 Wonders* be seen in all its glory. Blackstone did eventually take out another show, for his final tour of 1954–1955, but it was very different from the one we knew. There was no Sepoy Mutiny, no Princess Karnac levitation, no Elusive Moth. The golden age of the touring illusion show was over.

I am told that, before Mr. B performed his last vanishing act, he spent his days as the Grand Old Man of Magic at a new

Harry Blackstone, Sr. 1885 – 1965.

Hollywood club, The Magic Castle, which opened its doors in 1963. There, conversing with the club members or doing a bit of impromptu magic for guests, he had what I know was everything to him: an audience.

Blackstone died at the age of 80 on November 16, 1965.

The letter I received from Blackstone in 1950 was the last contact I had with the world of magic for more than half a century. I didn't even think about magic. My time as a box jumper was finished. I could no longer be a professional dancer. Show business was not the road I'd travel anymore. I had to find employment in some other line of work.

For a while, I was a waitress in a small restaurant near my

home. The year 1951 was fast approaching and I was about to meet someone, a man who worked in the kitchen at the restaurant. After knowing each other for only three months, we got married. A year later, in 1952, our first daughter was born. We named her Jean. Our second daughter, Louise, arrived in 1954. But our marriage went downhill and in 1956, we divorced.

Jean, Louise, and I accepted the invitation to move into the spacious home of my parents. My grandmother was already living there. With our taking up residence, there were four generations living under one roof. It was actually a good experience for all of us.

My dad was now lieutenant of police at the Philadelphia Naval Base. When my ankle finally healed, I was able to dance again. My father knew I couldn't make a career of it anymore, but he also knew what it meant to me to be able to get up and dance, so he made sure to volunteer me for all the variety shows at the naval base. The Navy Jazz Band provided the music.

During that same period, I donated my time to teaching young children to be confident in front of an audience — how to walk, turn around correctly, smile naturally, listen to the music, and enjoy moving onstage. I was also a member of a community theater group and, at the Plays & Players Theatre in Philadelphia's Center City, we did Off-Broadway musicals. I played the comedy lead in one of them: *Wake Up and Dance*.

In 1958, I was working as a waitress at the Merion Cricket Club. On an evening off — it was May 20, to be exact — I headed to Wagner's Ballroom in North Philadelphia. There, I could enjoy a night of dancing to the music of a live band. A man tapped me on the shoulder and asked me to dance. He turned out to be a fine gentleman named Bob Rhindress. It was a magical time for both of us and it didn't take long to know that we had something special. We dated for two years. Bob proposed marriage, I accepted, and in August 1960 we tied the knot.

Bob had his own television repair business. I had begun working as a secretary at Merck, Sharp & Dohme, a pharmaceutical company. When Bob and I found out that I was pregnant, we put a down-payment on a house in Blue Bell, Pennsylvania. In July 1961, our first son, Stephen, was born. I became a fulltime mom. We were a family of five. We had a new home. Bob opened a branch for his expanding business. Two more sons, Richard and Robert, were born in 1963 and 1964. We were a family of seven.

The next ten years were occupied with volunteer work in school libraries, being a math tutor, working as a newspaper reporter, being a Cub Scout Den Mother, and taking ice-dancing lessons so I could skate in the mornings while my children were in school.

My daughter Jean got married. In 1972, she had a son, Tom. My daughter Louise also wed, and she had a girl, Nikki, in 1980. My sons Steve, Rich, and Bob participated in orchestras, bands, and school stage shows, and then went to college to study music.

For twelve years, beginning in 1976, I was secretary to the president of a small company called Van Horn, Metz. Then, my dear husband became seriously ill with cancer. He passed away in 1983.

I was a widow at age 53, with three boys in college. How to make ends meet?

I started all over again, taking a better-paying secretarial job with Unisys, a computer company. My work permitted me to do what I had always wanted to do: go to college. I took night courses at Villanova University. I was 65, the oldest student there. But when my secretarial job moved to a different location, I could no longer pursue my studies at Villanova. I became a college drop-out.

In November 1999, at age 70, I retired from the company where I worked. But I never truly "retired" in the sense of spending all my time puttering around the house. I traveled quite a lot. As a member of the board of directors for the Philadelphia

Youth Orchestra, I was a chaperone for the group when they gave concerts in England, Scotland, Wales, Germany, Austria, Switzerland, Belgium, Argentina, Uruguay, and Brazil.

My sons graduated with Masters degrees in music. They got married and began families of their own. I have eight grandchildren now, and three great-grandchildren.

On November 13, 2004, my family gave me a surprise 75th birthday party. It was four days ahead of my actual birthday, so I had absolutely no clue. I was ushered into the restaurant banquet room, and there they were: my five children, their husbands and wives, their sons and daughters, my brother and his wife, my sister and her children, other family members, and a few neighbors. They were all applauding and yelling "Happy birthday!" I almost passed out.

Among the birthday gifts I received was something truly amazing. I was shown a nine-minute film clip of Harry Blackstone performing at the Hanna Theatre in Cleveland. I saw myself *eight times* in different costumes. I saw the Costume Trunk illusion from the audience perspective for the first time. I watched as I hopped out of the box, dressed as Little Red Riding Hood and wearing my toe shoes. Then, Blackstone extended his hand to take mine so he could twirl me around, just as he had done in real life. I was speechless. I didn't know such a film existed, yet it had been located through the hard detective work of my son Bob and his wife Erin. Suddenly, that long-ago magic experience came to life again.

A week later, at their home in Massachusetts, Bob and Erin arranged a surprise meeting with Nick Ruggiero. I hadn't seen Nick for 54 years. When I answered the door, I didn't recognize him — until he smiled. "Is that you, Nick?" I exclaimed. We spent six hours reliving the past, looking at photo albums, sharing stories about the magic days and what came after, and talking about Blackstone. I asked Nick if he ever went to magic conventions. "I go to all of them," he replied, and he suggested that I should plan to join him at the Magic Collectors Weekend convention in Las Vegas the following April.

That was the start of a new adventure for me. I have since been to many magic conventions, all across America, and even one at sea. I've met an astonishing number of magicians, who have all welcomed me with open arms. At gatherings of conjurors and magic aficionados, I'm treated as an honored guest, a rare connection to one of the greatest magic shows of the 20th century, and I've made many new friends.

To all the people who have shown so much kindness to me...

To my family, who brought magic back into my life...

I say a heartfelt thank you!

Before me, I see a door. It's not just any door. It's the *stage* door. I have walked through that doorway so many times, with dancers and musicians and stagehands, and with the world's greatest magician, Harry Blackstone.

Just inside is the stage doorman. He's the one who greets us when we arrive, takes messages for us, handles our mail, and acts as a security guard. The stage doorman always has a smile for us. When the day is done, he wishes us a good night as we exit the theater.

After everyone has gone, the stage doorman flicks on the ghost light, a single bulb that illuminates the empty stage. He makes sure the stage door is locked behind him. Then he leaves.

Until the matinee tomorrow.

Acknowledgments

These memoirs could not have come into being without the efforts and support of many people. First and foremost are my son Bob Rhindress and his wife Erin, who reached down the long corridor of time and brought out a part of my life I had kept in my mind but never really talked about. I still marvel over the fact that they were able to track down film footage of me performing onstage with Harry Blackstone. It was the crowning surprise of my 75th birthday party. To Bob and Erin, and to the rest of my family who pitched in to create that memorable occasion, I hope you know that you have what you have always had: my everlasting love and affection.

My reunion with Nick Ruggiero, also arranged by Bob and Erin, was not only delightful but providential. Nick kept a diary during his time with the Blackstone show. I, regrettably, had not. Nick deserves credit for numerous dates and places in these pages, as well as some of the photographs. Thanks, my friend, and best wishes to you always.

Daniel Waldron, my first editor, is the person who persuaded me that it would be worthwhile to put my memories on paper. Until Dan came along, I didn't think anyone would be interested in stories from my past. Thanks to his constant encouragement, my memories of the Blackstone show are in your hands. Dan, I hope you know how grateful I am for all of your help.

Gabe Fajuri, via his Squash Publishing enterprise, took on the task of ensuring that my memoirs would go out into the world so others could enjoy them. His devotion to magic, and to this project, is amazing to me.

David Parr was brought on board as final editor by our mutual friend, Gabe Fajuri. For David's ideas, his editorial guidance and his hard work, he has my thanks — as he does for our friendship.

While I was with the Blackstone show, I heard the music for the Chinese Fantasy hundreds of times, but could not remember the names of the tunes until they were given to me by the late Charles Reynolds, who knew them instantly. Charles and his wife Regina welcomed me back into the magic fold with great kindness. It is much appreciated.

Thanks are also due to Tom Ewing, Bill Rauscher, Dick and Joan Gustafson, Ann and Ray Goulet, and Terry Evanswood for their support. To Diego Domingo, thanks for writing about me in *Genii* magazine. To David and Anita Meyer, thanks for running an excerpt from my memoirs in *Magicol*.

Additional thanks go to Jim Alfredson, David Baldwin, Gay Blackstone, Trixie Bond, Mike Caveney, George Daily, Dennis Michael Dowhy, Jay Farrelly, Rod Hamer, Donna Horn, Max Howard, Paula Isenberg, Mac King, Bob Little, Joe Long, Max Maven, Mike Miller, John Moehring, Joe and Lisa Patire, Andy Martin Portala, Eduardo Nadur Sanchez, Jim Steinmeyer, Reba Strong, Teller, Frances Willard, and Ken Scott Wisenbaker for encouraging me along the way.

Magic is a fascinating art form practiced by remarkable people. No matter how you serve the magic muse — as performer, inventor, writer, publisher, consultant, collector, researcher, club member or club officer — you have my admiration.

Second from last was always the choicest position in vaudeville, and so it is here. To Dick Cavett, lifelong lover of magic, I offer my deepest thanks for his marvelous introduction, which perfectly captures the essence of what it was to fall under the spell of Blackstone.

Finally, I want to express how grateful I am to have been a part of that magical mirage, that chimera, that phantasmagoria called *Blackstone's Show of 1001 Wonders*. It gives me great joy to remember it. And I'm so happy to have had the opportunity to share that joy with readers before I, like the Elusive Moth, vanish completely into the dreaming air.

Blackstone Tour Routes

I joined the *Show of 1001 Wonders* during the first week of October 1947 and picked up show programs as I found them in theaters. Those programs provided some of the information in this list. Nick Ruggiero joined the show in January 1949 and kept a tour diary, so he was able to provide much additional information. Even so, we were unable to fill in all of the gaps in this list; some theaters, cities, and hotels are missing.

1947–1948 Season

Date	Theater	City	Hotel
Oct. 6	Walnut Street	Philadelphia, PA	
Oct. 20	Berkshire	Reading, PA	
Oct. 21	H.S. Auditorium	Lancaster, PA	
Oct. 22		Harrisburg, PA	
Oct. 25 - 26	Playhouse	Wilmington, DE	
Oct. 27 - Nov. 2	Nixon	Pittsburgh, PA	Fort Pitt
Nov. 3	Shea's	Bradford, PA	Holley
Nov. 4		Jamestown, NY	Samuels

Nov. 6 - 8	Park	Youngstown, OH	
Nov. 8	After the show, Herbie Washburn took Mr. B to hospital for a checkup.		
Nov. 9	Herbie drove Mr. B to Akron. No show. Mr. B rested.		
Nov. 10 - 11	Colonial	Akron, OH	Howe
Mr. B was too ill to perform after Nov 11. Tour canceled.			

1948–1949 Season

Date	Theater	City	Hotel
Aug. 18 - 25	Erlanger	Chicago, IL	Morrison
Aug. 26 - 28	Grand	London, Ont.	Belvedere
Aug. 30 - Sept. 10	Royal Alexandra	Toronto, Ont.	Canada Ford
Sept. 16	Shubert Lafayette	Detroit, MI	Barlum
Sept. 27 - Oct. 4	Davidson	Milwaukee, WI	Wisconsin
Oct. 5 - 6	Vocational School Auditorium	La Crosse, WI	Links
Oct. 7 - 9	St. Paul Auditorium	St. Paul, MN	
Oct. 10 - 17	Lyceum	Minneapolis, MN	Tallmadge
Oct. 18	KRNT Radio	Des Moines, IA	
Oct. 20 - 23	Music Hall	Kansas City, MO	Robert E. Lee
Oct. 24 - Nov. 7	American	St. Louis, MO	American
Nov. 8 - 14	Cox	Cincinnati, OH	
Nov. 15 - 20	Hartman	Columbus, OH	
Nov. 21	Auditorium	Dayton, OH	
Nov. 22 - 28	Hanna	Cleveland, OH	
Nov. 30 - Dec. 4	Nixon	Pittsburgh, PA	Fort Pitt
Dec. 6 - 12	Erlanger	Buffalo, NY	
Dec. 14 - 15	Strand	Elmira, NY	
Dec. 16 - 30	Colonial	Boston, MA	Avery
Jan. 1 - 22 1949	Walnut Street	Philadelphia, PA	

Jan. 23	War Memorial	Trenton, NJ	
Jan. 24	Rajah	Reading, PA	Berkshire
Jan. 25 - 26	Lyric	Allentown, PA	
Jan. 27 - 30	Playhouse	Wilmington, DE	Jepson
Jan. 31 - Feb. 6	Ford	Baltimore, MD	Congress
Feb. 8 - 9	Bushnell Memorial	Hartford, CT	
Feb. 10	Academy of Music	Northamton, MA	
Feb. 11 - 12	Erie	Schenectady, NY	
Feb. 14 - 19	His Majesty's	Montreal, QC	Queens
Feb. 20	Auditorium	Burlington, VT	
Feb. 21 - 26	Opera House	Newark, NJ	
Mar. 1 - 3	WRVA	Richmond, VA	
Mar. 4 - 5	Centre	Norfolk, VA	
Mar. 7 - 10	Murat	Indianapolis, IN	
Mar. 11 - 12	Coliseum	Evansville, IN	
Mar. 13 - 15	Memorial Auditorim	Louisville, KY	
Mar. 16	Grand Ole Opry	Nashville, TN	
Mar. 18 - 20	Ma Ellis Auditorium	Memphis, TN	
Mar. 21 - 24	Tower	Atlanta, GA	Georgian Ter.
On March 24, Mr. B. collapsed on the street and was rushed to the hospital. The remainder of the tour was canceled.			

1949–1950 Season

Date	Theater	City	Hotel
Sept. 9 - 10 (rehearsals)	Davidson	Milwaukee, WI	Belmont
Sept. 11 - 17	Davidson	Milwaukee, WI	Belmont
Sept. 19 - 22	Music Hall	Kansas City, MO	Robert E. Lee
Sept. 23 - 25	KRNT	Des Moines, IA	Franklin
Sept. 26 - 27	Auditorium	St. Joseph, MO	Jerome
Sept. 28	Memorial Hall	Salina, KS	Plains

Adele Friel Rhindress

Sept. 29	Arcadia	Wichita, KS	McClellan
Sept. 30 - Oct. 1	Convention Hall	Hutchinson, KS	Stamy
Oct. 2	Auditorium	Topeka, KS	Kansan
Oct. 4	Civic Center	Bartlesville, OK	Burlingame
Oct. 5	Home Theatre	Oklahoma City, OK	Hudson
Oct. 6	Convention Hall	Tulsa, OK	Reeder
Oct. 8	Shrine Mosque	Springfield, MO	Colonial
Oct. 9 - 22	American	St. Louis, MO	American
Oct. 24 - 29	Nixon	Pittsburgh, PA	Fort Pitt
Oct. 31 - Nov. 6	Hartman	Columbus, OH	Virginian
Nov. 7 - 13	Hanna	Cleveland, OH	Allerton/Earl
Nov. 14 - 16	Town Hall	Toledo, OH	Navarre
Nov. 17 - 19	Auditorium	Rochester, NY	Claridge
Nov. 21 - 27	Erlanger	Buffalo, NY	Huron
Nov. 29 - 30	Community Theater	Hershey, PA	
Dec. 1 - 4	Playhouse	Wilmington, DE	Olivere
Dec. 5 -10, 12 - 17	Walnut Street	Philadelphia, PA	
Dec. 26 - Jan. 1	Ford	Baltimore, MD	Biltmore
Jan. 2 - 4	WREA	Richmond, VA	
Jan. 5 - 7	Auditorium	Charleston, WV	Barker
Jan 8 - 11	Murat	Indianapolis, IN	Barton
Jan. 12 - 15	Auditorium	Louisville, KY	Colonial
Jan. 16 - 17	Henry Clay Auditorium	Lexington, KY	Drake
Jan. 20 - 22	Auditorium	Memphis, TN	Arlington
Jan. 23 - 29	Poche	New Orleans, LA	LaSalle
Jan. 30 - 31	Murphy Audit.	Mobile, AL	La Clide
Feb. 2 - 4	Tower	Atlanta, GA	Hampton
Feb. 6	Lanier HS Auditorium	Montgomery, AL	Exchange
Feb. 7	Temple	Birmingham, AL	Hillman
Feb. 10 -11	Robinson Auditorium	Little Rock, AR	New Capitol

116 | *Memoirs of an Elusive Moth*

Feb. 19 - Mar. 11	Erlanger	Chicago, IL	Croydon
Mar. 13 - 19	Shubert Lafayette	Detroit, MI	Barlum
Mar. 20 - 21, 23 - 26	RKO Keiths	Grand Rapis, MI	Earle
Mar. 27 - 28	State	Kalamazoo, MI	Milner
Mar. 29	Bijou	Battle Creek, MI	Post Tavern
Mar. 30	Palace	Flint, MI	Reed
Mar. 31	Temple	Saginaw, MI	Roberts
Apr. 1	Washington	Bay City, MI	Republic

UPPER MERION TOWNSHIP LIBRARY
175 WEST VALLEY FORGE ROAD
KING OF PRUSSIA, PA 19406

ADULT DEPT. - (610) 265-4805
CHILDREN'S DEPT. - (610) 265-4806

3/30/15